This journal belongs to

Dedication
With all my love; to my mum Patricia, my constant through all the
changing cycles of life and my darling Samuel,
my shining light and north star.

www.louisecroker.com
Facebook: @thewilgatree
Send feedback to
louise@louisecroker.com
ISBN-978-0-646-82518-2

Contents

4

Acknowledgement of Country

I acknowledge and pay respect to all Australian Aboriginal people, the traditional custodians of the land on which I live, in particular to the Dharawal people on whose country this journal was created.

As original custodians of this land I pay respect to Elders past, present and emerging, and give thanks to the land and to the peoples and culture who cared for, respected and honoured this beautiful country for tens of thousands of years before the invasion of colonisation.

May we learn from you, may we come back to your wisdom, and may we one day honour and care for this land as you have always done.

Introduction

Welcome to the My Moon Journal 2021

The moon in her capricious ways demonstrates her independence and wilfulness by creating her own time and movement through the skies; unlike her solar brother's calendar with its structured seven-day weeks, 4-5 week months and 12 month year.

The moon's lunar year is instead made up of 13 cycles, with each new year beginning on a different date within the solar calendar. Throughout these 13 cycles the moon moves through four major phases: new moon, first quarter moon, full moon and third quarter moon, with each phase and each cycle being of varying duration in length.

This constantly changing movement is why it is so hard to fully connect with the deeply soulful nature of the lunar year through a regular solar diary.

Therefore, the My Moon Journal has been designed to track your year through these 13 cycles and through the four major moon phases within each cycle, clearly displaying the day and dates of each phase of the moon and each lunar cycle.

For the journal to sit neatly into the solar calendar year, an additional '14th' cycle, being the 13 cycle from the previous lunar year, has been added before the start of the 2021 Lunar New Year (Friday 12 February). This cycle can also be used as a 'practice' run for using the lunar cycles ahead.

As this Journal has been created in Australia, there may be some slight differences (no more than 24hrs) in the dates for your area depending on where you are in the world. Where possible I have tried to accommodate broadly for both the Southern and Northern Hemispheres.

I hope you enjoy your journey with the 2021 My Moon Journal.

Blessings
Louise Croker

Testimonials

I've really enjoyed using the My Moon Journal this year. I like being more in tune with what is occurring as the moon moves through its cycles, and more consciously working with the manifestation and release phases.
Robyn L, Queensland, Australia, 2020

This year's journal has kept me sane.
Alison B, New South Wales, Australia, 2020

Moon Blessing

Sister moon I receive your blessing, opening my heart, mind, body and soul to your light.

May your cyclic influence move in time with my own, ebbing and flowing in gentle harmony.

May this connection move me to accept and embrace the rhythms and nature of my body, the needs and desires of my heart, the power and wisdom of my soul.

May I come to know and understand my need for closeness, alongside my desire for distance.

May I be willing and able to step into my power and strength and when required, my gentleness and vulnerability.

May I know and accept my inner call and need for self care, in equal measure to the need for service to my community.

Help me to know when it is time for me to shine, but also when it is time to move into darkness.

Help me to use my power in the gentle ways of care and kindness as I move within the landscape of my life, and when needed, grant me the courage to bring about change, sweeping away all that no longer serves me.

Grant me the freedom and courage to allow flow, giving myself permission to be moved by the tides, and trust in Love to bring opportunities again and again for my transformation and growth.

May I never play small with my soul, instead step boldly into it, opening and serving fully from my heart.

Amen

Why Journal

Journals and diaries have been written and kept for centuries. While early journals and diaries recorded the happenings of public life, these days they are a personal tool that help us to externalise our internal world, in a way that feels private and safe. Journaling has many benefits for health and wellbeing and is a tool to express emotion, detox the mind, verbalise the unsayable and to record that which is worthy of holding in memory.

Some of the many benefits of journaling are:

To Gain Clarity: Just as a mirror reflects back to you your body, journaling provides a glimpse into the working of both your conscious and subconscious mind and heart. Journaling provides a record of who you are, how you think and what you feel, increasing your awareness of everything about both your inner and outer worlds.

To Strengthen Emotional Understanding: Journaling can help us to become more resilient and able to identify our strengths as we deal with personal hurt and change, as well as emphasising important patterns and areas of growth in life. Expressive writing can help us to develop deeper understandings about ourselves, others, and the world around us, helping us to understand and feel comfortable within our own emotional landscape, while also teaching us how we can best process our responses to life's challenges. Journaling can also help us to see other perspectives and view situations through a different lens, increasing our capacity for empathy and understanding of other's circumstances and behaviours.

To Feel Calmer: Journaling allows us privacy and provides a safe place to express our true inner self, as our journal is for our eyes only to see. Through writing we let go of intense feelings helping to prevent us getting stuck in a mental or emotional loop and experiencing unnecessary suffering. Expressing our emotions in writing helps to release them, allowing us to feel lighter, calmer and less stressed.

To Solve Problems: Sometimes the only way we can arrive at the answer to a problem is by tapping into our creative, intuitive and emotional right-brain which is precisely what journaling does. Through journaling techniques such as free writing we can help to unlock creative solutions we might never have thought of before.

To Increase Creativity: The creative side of journaling can also spill into other areas of our life by giving us the courage to try new creative skills and mediums. Once we get rolling, our muse takes over and like journaling, we gain the courage to try out new ideas without fear of judgment.

To Boost Memory and Cognition: Journaling helps keep our brain in shape. Not only does it boost memory and comprehension, it also increases our working memory capacity, which can lead to improved cognitive processing. Journaling does this by helping us to organize our thoughts and memory through presenting them clearly on paper.

To Track Patterns: When we journal, we often find ourselves covering the same territory over and over again, which is often only fully realised when we look back on earlier entries. These may be negative thoughts and behaviours we have identified or certain people or events that trigger us. By zeroing in on the problem, we then create an opportunity to make positive changes in our life.

How to use this journal

Each part of the My Moon Journal offers a different way to explore and connect with your inner life, your soul, your highest wisdom. While the My Moon Journal takes you through a journey from one year into the next and offers guidance and information on how you might undertake that journey, at the end of the day this journey, and this journal is your own. It is a place to open up to your private and most inner self, a place to be honest, wholehearted and authentic, and to that end, how you use it up to you.

If you choose to follow the journey offered, I provide the following guidance to navigate the My Moon Journal and wish you many blessings for the year ahead.

The My Moon Journal is made up of five sections:
- 13th Cycle from the 2020 My Moon Journal,
- closing the 2020 Lunar Year,
- the 2021 Lunar New Year,
- My Cycle,
- and Journaling.

Each section provides the opportunity to reflect and to centre. These opportunities are a time to pause and review your life, your feelings, your experiences, and your expectations. What is presented before you is a time to own for yourself. This is your sacred space and time, that allows for review and change and also peace and consolidation. The more that you treat it as such, the more you will get out of this process.

13th Cycle 2020

This is the thirteenth cycle of the 2020 lunar year, it aligns this journal with the solar calendar year and provides you with an opportunity to play and experiment with how you might use the journal going forward.

Closing the 2020 Lunar Year

This is an important section to help free yourself of anything that may be holding you back, or for bringing to your awareness anything that needs to be acknowledged and healed going forward. It is also a time to reflect on and re-enjoy happy experiences, consolidating them in your memory for future reference. Tell your personal stories here, take time to reflect and feel into what needs healing, what needs remembering and what needs letting go.

2021 Lunar New Year

The 2021 Lunar New Year is a section of self-reflection and intention setting for the coming lunar year. It offers twenty-four questions across twelve key areas of life, encouraging you to explore in some depth how you would like to show up and engage with life in 2021. Here is the opportunity to start the creation process for a brilliant new lunar year.

My Cycle

Whether male or female, menstruating or menopausal, all bodies, minds, hearts, and energy systems travel through a cycle of reoccurring changes. By using the My Cycle section to track your feelings, moods, energy changes and physical experiences throughout each lunar cycle, you will become more aware of some of the patterns and rhythms of your life, and you may be surprised by what it reveals.

Journaling

This is the area for your thoughts, reflections, feelings, and memories. Each lunar cycle is broken into sections to inform and support your journaling process. Each cycle includes pages for; New Moon manifesting, First Quarter Moon power up, Full Moon celebration, Third Quarter Moon releasing, and daily journaling. Each section also contains journaling prompts and information to help you get started.

If you are interested in astrology and a more intimate connection with the land, you will also find information on:

- periods of mercury in retrograde,
- lunar eclipses
- seasonal equinox and solstices, and
- the full moon names.

The Changing Faces of the Moon

Each phase of the moon brings with it a particular energy frequency, which through our reflection and journaling we can make the most of to manifest a life that is intentional, authentic and abundant. By becoming more in touch with our own internal rhythms and with the rhythms of the land and the skies we can become more connected with our purpose, desires, strengths, and ability to heal ourselves and our world.

New Moon, New Beginnings

Now is the time to gather your thoughts and plan. The New Moon is the time of fresh starts, new beginnings, growth, optimism and starting over. In these few days ahead seize the opportunity to review, change, enhance or refocus your attention and intentions on an area or areas of your life in which you want to manifest your desires.

First Quarter Moon, Moving Forward

This is the time for moving forward with your intentions, desires and plans, a time for taking action. The waxing energy is gaining strength and powering you forward. It is the perfect time for accomplishments, creativity, strength, growth, learning, and positive transformation.

Full Moon, The Harvest

The Full Moon is the time when the moon's energy is at its peak, it is a time of celebration and of reaping the harvest of your previous New Moons intentions. Learning the art and vulnerability of opening yourself to receiving abundance, the harvest, achievement, and protection is powerful at this time.

Third Quarter Moon, Letting Go

The Third Quarter Moon is the time of releasing anything standing in your way. Letting go of old patterns, behaviours, thoughts, and emotions. A time to recognise and release anything that no longer serves your highest good in preparation for the manifesting period of the next New Moon.

Eclipses:

Eclipses, whether solar or lunar, demand that we move forward. Lunar eclipses in particular are times for emotion-based endings, a time for revealing and healing old woundings and a time for letting go of the past. It is important at these times to reflect on and acknowledge what is arising and through gratitude release what needs to be set free so that we can face our future with nothing impeding our forward movement. This time can also simply be a time of sentimentality and reliving old memories. The degree of impact each eclipse has will be dependent on how close it is to your astrological natal chart and birth sign.

Full Moon Names

Each cycle includes a different name for the full moon. There are many cultures and times with traditions for full moon naming including, Celtic, Medieval, Native American, and Chinese. For some cultures there are also much deeper meanings and significance than the name and descriptions I have included in the My Moon Journal. It is neither my place nor desire to appropriate these deeper meanings for the purposes of this journal, therefore the descriptions I have included are simply reflections on how mother earth is showing herself at these changing times of the year.

To date I have been unable to find Indigenous Australian descriptions, however that does not mean they don't exist, only that that I don't have access to them, and that may be as is should be. Instead I have used suggestions provided by Springwolf[1] who has explored the changing seasons on mother earth in the southern hemisphere and suggested names accordingly. The northern hemisphere names and descriptions have been taken from the Thomas Old Farmer's Almanac founded in America in 1792. The almanac used names that were widely used in Scotland, Ireland, England, France and most of their territories, and was also influenced by the full moon names used by Native American Indian culture.

Mercury in Retrograde

Despite what the term retrograde implies, planets don't really go backwards, all the planets in our solar system move in the same continuous direction around the Sun. Rather, in the context of astrology the word retrograde refers to an optical illusion where it sometimes appears that a planet will stop and go backwards, and then stop again and go forwards. The planet Mercury does this three times each calendar year, with often profound effects for those sensitive to it.

There are three parts to a Mercury in Retrograde, pre, full, and post. As Mercury appears to slow down before the retrograde, this is called the pre-retrograde, then as Mercury appears to pick up speed or gain forward momentum again this is the post-retrograde period. The most impactful time is during the full retrograde, however its effects may still be felt both before and after.

Mercury in Retrograde has tended to get a bad rap, especially in our busy, must get things done at all costs world, as during this period it often appears as though things are going wrong, we can feel as though one obstacle after another is being placed in

---

[1] https://springwolf.net

front of us, and if we are unaware of what is happening in our skies our lives may feel disrupted and chaotic for no apparent reason.

But, Mercury in Retrograde offers us a blessing as it is all about slowing down, being more mindful and focusing on quality not quantity. Our modern mindset often forces us to constantly be on the go, rarely stopping to relax and be truly present. We jump from one project to the next in an attempt to accomplish something new or better, but this urge to do more can prevent us from being thorough in the work that we do undertake. So often we don't strive to get things done right, but just to get them done.

Mercury in Retrograde offers us a chance to slow down, go back to our previous work, and tie up loose ends. Be they from projects, relationships, unhealed emotions, old memories, communications, or tasks. When we choose to embrace this opportunity, we become more aligned with the energies present and flow with the current rather than fighting against it. Ultimately, by going retrograde ourselves (going back over our work), we will avoid many of the pitfalls normally associated with this period in the planetary cycle.

Just as the tides allow themselves to be influenced by the pull of the moon, allow yourself to use the pull of Mercury in Retrograde as a welcome reprieve from the crazy break-neck pace that society requires us to take during the rest of the year.

You will find the dates for each Mercury in Retrograde at the top of your journaling pages, including the pre and post periods and the star sign in which the retrograde is operating.

The Changing Seasons

As we begin to attune to the movement of the heavens oft times our awareness can also turn to the changes of a more earthly nature, the most prominent of these being the changing seasons. For this reason, I have also included within the moon cycles the Druidic seasonal celebrations[2] of:

- Alban Eilir, the Spring Equinox
- Alban Hefin, the Summer Solstice
- Alban Elfed, the Autumn Equinox
- Alban Arthan, the Winter Solstice
- Beltane, the beginning of Summer
- Samhain (Halloween), the beginning of Winter

---

[2] https://druidry.org/

To find out more about the significance and celebrations that go with each of these seasons, one source of information is www.druidry.org.

Closing the 2020 Lunar Year

Lunar Cycle 13

Wednesday 13 January to Thursday 11 February 2021
Final cycle from 2020

New Moon Manifesting

New Beginnings

Wednesday 13 January 2021 – Southern
Wednesday 13 January 2021 – Northern

What are my intentions for the coming lunar cycle?

- Physical Health
- Mental and Cognitive Health
- `Abundance and Lifestyle
- Safety and Security
- Environment
- Play
- Authenticity
- Communication
- Relationships
- Self-Responsibility and Growth
- Community
- Finding Meaning

My Faith:

Use this section for a card reading, bible verse or quote that speaks to you.

My Journaling

Wednesday 13 January to Wednesday 20 January 2021 - Southern
Wednesday 13 January to Tuesday 19 January 2021 – Northern

Mercury in Retrograde: Pre: 14 to 30 January in Aquarius

New Moon
Wed 13 Jan

Journaling prompt: The words I'd like to live by are...

First Quarter Moon Power Up

Moving Forward
Thursday 21 January 2021 – Southern
Wednesday 20 January 2021 – Northern

What actions will I take now to move my intentions forward?

- Physical Health
- Mental and Cognitive Health
- Abundance and Lifestyle
- Safety and Security
- Environment
- Play
- Authenticity
- Communication
- Relationships
- Self-Responsibility and Growth
- Community
- Finding Meaning

My Journaling

Thursday 21 January to Wednesday 27 January 2021 - Southern
Wednesday 20 January to Wednesday 27 January 2021 – Northern

Mercury in Retrograde: Pre: 14 to 30 January in Aquarius

First Quarter Moon
Thurs 21 Jan
Wed 20 Jan

Journaling prompt: When I'm in pain (physical or emotional) the kindest thing I can do for myself is...

Full Moon Celebration

The Harvest
Thursday 28 January 2021 – Southern
Thursday 28 January 2021 – Northern

What am I celebrating and reaping the harvest of this Full Moon?

- Physical Health
- Mental and Cognitive Health
- Abundance and Lifestyle
- Safety and Security
- Environment
- Play
- Authenticity
- Communication
- Relationships
- Self-Responsibility and Growth
- Community
- Finding Meaning

The full moon in January

The Thunder Moon in the **Southern Hemisphere;** is the time thunderstorms are most frequent. This first full moon in the calendar year could also be called the Rumble Moon or the Lightning Moon.

The Hunger Moon in the **Northern Hemisphere;** in cold and temperate climates, it was difficult to find food during January, thus the name hunger moon.

My Journaling

Thursday 28 January to Thursday 4 February 2021 - Southern
Thursday 28 January to Wednesday 3 February 2021 - Northern

Mercury in Retrograde: Full: 31 January to 21 February in Aquarius

Full Moon
Thurs 28 Jan

Journaling prompt: If my body could talk, it would say...

Third Quarter Moon Releasing

Letting It Go

Friday 5 February 2021 – Southern
Thursday 4 February 2021 – Northern

At this time of the Third Quarter Moon I see, acknowledge and release...

- Physical Health
- Mental and Cognitive Health
- Abundance and Lifestyle
- Safety and Security
- Environment
- Play
- Authenticity
- Communication
- Relationships
- Self-Responsibility and Growth
- Community
- Finding Meaning

My Journaling

Thursday 5 February to Thursday 11 February 2021 - Southern
Wednesday 4 February to Wednesday 10 February 2021 - Northern

Mercury in Retrograde: Full: 31 January to 21 February in Aquarius

Third Quarter
Moon
Fri 5 Feb
Thurs 4 Feb

Journaling prompt: Nobody knows that 1 . . .

Closing the
2020 Lunar Year

End of Lunar Year Closing

As the 2020 Lunar Year closes, now is the time to reflect on the year that has just been. Honouring ourselves with taking time to reflect on and process our feelings and experiences from 2020 and creating a pause between what has been and what will be.

In doing so, we allow a process of decluttering to start, creating space for something new and different to emerge.

Bring patience and gentleness to this time in the liminal, connecting to what needs healing before turning to what is waiting to be born. Celebrate what has been learnt, healed, and accomplished throughout the 2020 lunar year and allow yourself to breathe.

What feelings arise when I think back on the 2020 lunar year?

What are these feelings connected to?

What did I change in 2020? How did I change in 2020?

How are am I living my life differently because of 2020?

What are some important memories from 2020?

Following this time spent time in reflecting on what has been, if you have a copy of the 2020 My Moon Journal, now is the time to go back and read through your 2020 Annual Review section.

My Cycle

How to Track my Cycles

Whether male or female, menstruating or menopausal, all bodies, minds, hearts, and energy systems travel through a cycle of reoccurring changes.

By using the My Cycle section, you can track your feelings, moods, energy changes and physical experiences throughout each lunar cycle. Through this process you will become aware of your own patterns and rhythms, how they relate to the cycles and phases of the moon and how they effect and impact your life.

Tracking my rhythms

A numbering system is provided in the My Cycle section to track your changes; however, you may prefer to use your own system of words, symbols or numbers.

Emotion	Distressing Feelings 1 2 3 4 5	Heightened and Blissful Feelings
Physical Body	Distress in the body 1 2 3 4 5	Comfort and Wellness
Energy	Tight and closed 1 2 3 4 5	Light and open
Mental	Sluggish and slow 1 2 3 4 5	High speed
Head or Heart	In the Head 1 2 3 4 5	In the heart

How you choose to use this section is entirely up to you, the numbering system has been made deliberately grey so that it can be written over with words, images or symbols.

Cycle 13 (end of 2020 lunar year)

New Moon	First Quarter Moon	Full Moon	Last Quarter Moon
Wed 13 Jan	**Thurs 21 Jan**	**Thurs 28 Jan**	**Fri 5 Feb**
Emotion 1 2 3 4 5	Emotion 1 2 3 4 5	Emotion 1 2 3 4 5	Emotion 1 2 3 4 5
Physical 1 2 3 4 5	Physical 1 2 3 4 5	Physical 1 2 3 4 5	Physical 1 2 3 4 5
Energy 1 2 3 4 5	Energy 1 2 3 4 5	Energy 1 2 3 4 5	Energy 1 2 3 4 5
Mental 1 2 3 4 5	Mental 1 2 3 4 5	Mental 1 2 3 4 5	Mental 1 2 3 4 5
Head/Heart 1 2 3 4 5	Head/Heart 1 2 3 4 5	Head/Heart 1 2 3 4 5	Head/Heart 1 2 3 4 5
Thurs 14 Jan	**Fri 22 Jan**	**Fri 29 Jan**	**Sat 6 Feb**
Emotion 1 2 3 4 5	Emotion 1 2 3 4 5	Emotion 1 2 3 4 5	Emotion 1 2 3 4 5
Physical 1 2 3 4 5	Physical 1 2 3 4 5	Physical 1 2 3 4 5	Physical 1 2 3 4 5
Energy 1 2 3 4 5	Energy 1 2 3 4 5	Energy 1 2 3 4 5	Energy 1 2 3 4 5
Mental 1 2 3 4 5	Mental 1 2 3 4 5	Mental 1 2 3 4 5	Mental 1 2 3 4 5
Head/Heart 1 2 3 4 5	Head/Heart 1 2 3 4 5	Head/Heart 1 2 3 4 5	Head/Heart 1 2 3 4 5
Fri 15 Jan	**Sat 23 Jan**	**Sat 30 Jan**	**Sun 7 Feb**
Emotion 1 2 3 4 5	Emotion 1 2 3 4 5	Emotion 1 2 3 4 5	Emotion 1 2 3 4 5
Physical 1 2 3 4 5	Physical 1 2 3 4 5	Physical 1 2 3 4 5	Physical 1 2 3 4 5
Energy 1 2 3 4 5	Energy 1 2 3 4 5	Energy 1 2 3 4 5	Energy 1 2 3 4 5
Mental 1 2 3 4 5	Mental 1 2 3 4 5	Mental 1 2 3 4 5	Mental 1 2 3 4 5
Head/Heart 1 2 3 4 5	Head/Heart 1 2 3 4 5	Head/Heart 1 2 3 4 5	Head/Heart 1 2 3 4 5
Sat 16 Jan	**Sun 24 Jan**	**Sun 31 Jan**	**Mon 8 Feb**
Emotion 1 2 3 4 5	Emotion 1 2 3 4 5	Emotion 1 2 3 4 5	Emotion 1 2 3 4 5
Physical 1 2 3 4 5	Physical 1 2 3 4 5	Physical 1 2 3 4 5	Physical 1 2 3 4 5
Energy 1 2 3 4 5	Energy 1 2 3 4 5	Energy 1 2 3 4 5	Energy 1 2 3 4 5
Mental 1 2 3 4 5	Mental 1 2 3 4 5	Mental 1 2 3 4 5	Mental 1 2 3 4 5
Head/Heart 1 2 3 4 5	Head/Heart 1 2 3 4 5	Head/Heart 1 2 3 4 5	Head/Heart 1 2 3 4 5
Sun 17 Jan	**Mon 25 Jan**	**Mon 1 Feb**	**Tues 9 Feb**
Emotion 1 2 3 4 5	Emotion 1 2 3 4 5	Emotion 1 2 3 4 5	Emotion 1 2 3 4 5
Physical 1 2 3 4 5	Physical 1 2 3 4 5	Physical 1 2 3 4 5	Physical 1 2 3 4 5
Energy 1 2 3 4 5	Energy 1 2 3 4 5	Energy 1 2 3 4 5	Energy 1 2 3 4 5
Mental 1 2 3 4 5	Mental 1 2 3 4 5	Mental 1 2 3 4 5	Mental 1 2 3 4 5
Head/Heart 1 2 3 4 5	Head/Heart 1 2 3 4 5	Head/Heart 1 2 3 4 5	Head/Heart 1 2 3 4 5
Mon 18 Jan	**Tues 26 Jan**	**Tues 2 Feb**	**Wed 10 Feb**
Emotion 1 2 3 4 5	Emotion 1 2 3 4 5	Emotion 1 2 3 4 5	Emotion 1 2 3 4 5
Physical 1 2 3 4 5	Physical 1 2 3 4 5	Physical 1 2 3 4 5	Physical 1 2 3 4 5
Energy 1 2 3 4 5	Energy 1 2 3 4 5	Energy 1 2 3 4 5	Energy 1 2 3 4 5
Mental 1 2 3 4 5	Mental 1 2 3 4 5	Mental 1 2 3 4 5	Mental 1 2 3 4 5
Head/Heart 1 2 3 4 5	Head/Heart 1 2 3 4 5	Head/Heart 1 2 3 4 5	Head/Heart 1 2 3 4 5
Tues 19 Jan	**Wed 27 Jan**	**Wed 3 Feb**	**Thurs 11 Feb**
Emotion 1 2 3 4 5	Emotion 1 2 3 4 5	Emotion 1 2 3 4 5	Emotion 1 2 3 4 5
Physical 1 2 3 4 5	Physical 1 2 3 4 5	Physical 1 2 3 4 5	Physical 1 2 3 4 5
Energy 1 2 3 4 5	Energy 1 2 3 4 5	Energy 1 2 3 4 5	Energy 1 2 3 4 5
Mental 1 2 3 4 5	Mental 1 2 3 4 5	Mental 1 2 3 4 5	Mental 1 2 3 4 5
Head/Heart 1 2 3 4 5	Head/Heart 1 2 3 4 5	Head/Heart 1 2 3 4 5	Head/Heart 1 2 3 4 5
Wed 20 Jan	**Wed 27 Jan**	**Thurs 4 Feb**	**Thurs 11 Feb**
Emotion 1 2 3 4 5	Emotion 1 2 3 4 5	Emotion 1 2 3 4 5	Emotion 1 2 3 4 5
Physical 1 2 3 4 5	Physical 1 2 3 4 5	Physical 1 2 3 4 5	Physical 1 2 3 4 5
Energy 1 2 3 4 5	Energy 1 2 3 4 5	Energy 1 2 3 4 5	Energy 1 2 3 4 5
Mental 1 2 3 4 5	Mental 1 2 3 4 5	Mental 1 2 3 4 5	Mental 1 2 3 4 5
Head/Heart 1 2 3 4 5	Head/Heart 1 2 3 4 5	Head/Heart 1 2 3 4 5	Head/Heart 1 2 3 4 5

Cycle 1

New Moon	First Quarter Moon	Full Moon	Last Quarter Moon
Fri 12 Feb	**Sat 20 Feb**	**Sat 27 Feb**	**Sat 6 Mar**
Emotion 1 2 3 4 5 Physical 1 2 3 4 5 Energy 1 2 3 4 5 Mental 1 2 3 4 5 Head/Heart 1 2 3 4 5	Emotion 1 2 3 4 5 Physical 1 2 3 4 5 Energy 1 2 3 4 5 Mental 1 2 3 4 5 Head/Heart 1 2 3 4 5	Emotion 1 2 3 4 5 Physical 1 2 3 4 5 Energy 1 2 3 4 5 Mental 1 2 3 4 5 Head/Heart 1 2 3 4 5	Emotion 1 2 3 4 5 Physical 1 2 3 4 5 Energy 1 2 3 4 5 Mental 1 2 3 4 5 Head/Heart 1 2 3 4 5
Sat 13 Feb	**Sun 21 Feb**	**Sun 28 Feb**	**Sun 7 Mar**
Emotion 1 2 3 4 5 Physical 1 2 3 4 5 Energy 1 2 3 4 5 Mental 1 2 3 4 5 Head/Heart 1 2 3 4 5	Emotion 1 2 3 4 5 Physical 1 2 3 4 5 Energy 1 2 3 4 5 Mental 1 2 3 4 5 Head/Heart 1 2 3 4 5	Emotion 1 2 3 4 5 Physical 1 2 3 4 5 Energy 1 2 3 4 5 Mental 1 2 3 4 5 Head/Heart 1 2 3 4 5	Emotion 1 2 3 4 5 Physical 1 2 3 4 5 Energy 1 2 3 4 5 Mental 1 2 3 4 5 Head/Heart 1 2 3 4 5
Sun 14 Feb	**Mon 22 Feb**	**Mon 1 Mar**	**Mon 8 Mar**
Emotion 1 2 3 4 5 Physical 1 2 3 4 5 Energy 1 2 3 4 5 Mental 1 2 3 4 5 Head/Heart 1 2 3 4 5	Emotion 1 2 3 4 5 Physical 1 2 3 4 5 Energy 1 2 3 4 5 Mental 1 2 3 4 5 Head/Heart 1 2 3 4 5	Emotion 1 2 3 4 5 Physical 1 2 3 4 5 Energy 1 2 3 4 5 Mental 1 2 3 4 5 Head/Heart 1 2 3 4 5	Emotion 1 2 3 4 5 Physical 1 2 3 4 5 Energy 1 2 3 4 5 Mental 1 2 3 4 5 Head/Heart 1 2 3 4 5
Mon 15 Feb	**Tues 23 Feb**	**Tues 2 Mar**	**Tues 9 Mar**
Emotion 1 2 3 4 5 Physical 1 2 3 4 5 Energy 1 2 3 4 5 Mental 1 2 3 4 5 Head/Heart 1 2 3 4 5	Emotion 1 2 3 4 5 Physical 1 2 3 4 5 Energy 1 2 3 4 5 Mental 1 2 3 4 5 Head/Heart 1 2 3 4 5	Emotion 1 2 3 4 5 Physical 1 2 3 4 5 Energy 1 2 3 4 5 Mental 1 2 3 4 5 Head/Heart 1 2 3 4 5	Emotion 1 2 3 4 5 Physical 1 2 3 4 5 Energy 1 2 3 4 5 Mental 1 2 3 4 5 Head/Heart 1 2 3 4 5
Tues 16 Feb	**Wed 24 Feb**	**Wed 3 Mar**	**Wed 10 Mar**
Emotion 1 2 3 4 5 Physical 1 2 3 4 5 Energy 1 2 3 4 5 Mental 1 2 3 4 5 Head/Heart 1 2 3 4 5	Emotion 1 2 3 4 5 Physical 1 2 3 4 5 Energy 1 2 3 4 5 Mental 1 2 3 4 5 Head/Heart 1 2 3 4 5	Emotion 1 2 3 4 5 Physical 1 2 3 4 5 Energy 1 2 3 4 5 Mental 1 2 3 4 5 Head/Heart 1 2 3 4 5	Emotion 1 2 3 4 5 Physical 1 2 3 4 5 Energy 1 2 3 4 5 Mental 1 2 3 4 5 Head/Heart 1 2 3 4 5
Wed 17 Feb	**Thurs 25 Feb**	**Thurs 4 Mar**	**Thurs 11 Mar**
Emotion 1 2 3 4 5 Physical 1 2 3 4 5 Energy 1 2 3 4 5 Mental 1 2 3 4 5 Head/Heart 1 2 3 4 5	Emotion 1 2 3 4 5 Physical 1 2 3 4 5 Energy 1 2 3 4 5 Mental 1 2 3 4 5 Head/Heart 1 2 3 4 5	Emotion 1 2 3 4 5 Physical 1 2 3 4 5 Energy 1 2 3 4 5 Mental 1 2 3 4 5 Head/Heart 1 2 3 4 5	Emotion 1 2 3 4 5 Physical 1 2 3 4 5 Energy 1 2 3 4 5 Mental 1 2 3 4 5 Head/Heart 1 2 3 4 5
Thurs 18 Feb	**Fri 26 Feb**	**Fri 5 Mar**	**Fri 12 Mar**
Emotion 1 2 3 4 5 Physical 1 2 3 4 5 Energy 1 2 3 4 5 Mental 1 2 3 4 5 Head/Heart 1 2 3 4 5	Emotion 1 2 3 4 5 Physical 1 2 3 4 5 Energy 1 2 3 4 5 Mental 1 2 3 4 5 Head/Heart 1 2 3 4 5	Emotion 1 2 3 4 5 Physical 1 2 3 4 5 Energy 1 2 3 4 5 Mental 1 2 3 4 5 Head/Heart 1 2 3 4 5	Emotion 1 2 3 4 5 Physical 1 2 3 4 5 Energy 1 2 3 4 5 Mental 1 2 3 4 5 Head/Heart 1 2 3 4 5
Fri 19 Feb			
Emotion 1 2 3 4 5 Physical 1 2 3 4 5 Energy 1 2 3 4 5 Mental 1 2 3 4 5 Head/Heart 1 2 3 4 5			

Cycle 2

New Moon	First Quarter Moon	Full Moon	Last Quarter Moon
Sat 13 Mar	**Mon 22 Mar**	**Mon 29 Mar**	**Sun 4 April**
Emotion 1 2 3 4 5 Physical 1 2 3 4 5 Energy 1 2 3 4 5 Mental 1 2 3 4 5 Head/Heart 1 2 3 4 5	Emotion 1 2 3 4 5 Physical 1 2 3 4 5 Energy 1 2 3 4 5 Mental 1 2 3 4 5 Head/Heart 1 2 3 4 5	Emotion 1 2 3 4 5 Physical 1 2 3 4 5 Energy 1 2 3 4 5 Mental 1 2 3 4 5 Head/Heart 1 2 3 4 5	Emotion 1 2 3 4 5 Physical 1 2 3 4 5 Energy 1 2 3 4 5 Mental 1 2 3 4 5 Head/Heart 1 2 3 4 5
Sun 14 Mar	**Tues 23 Mar**	**Tues 30 Mon**	**Mon 5 April**
Emotion 1 2 3 4 5 Physical 1 2 3 4 5 Energy 1 2 3 4 5 Mental 1 2 3 4 5 Head/Heart 1 2 3 4 5	Emotion 1 2 3 4 5 Physical 1 2 3 4 5 Energy 1 2 3 4 5 Mental 1 2 3 4 5 Head/Heart 1 2 3 4 5	Emotion 1 2 3 4 5 Physical 1 2 3 4 5 Energy 1 2 3 4 5 Mental 1 2 3 4 5 Head/Heart 1 2 3 4 5	Emotion 1 2 3 4 5 Physical 1 2 3 4 5 Energy 1 2 3 4 5 Mental 1 2 3 4 5 Head/Heart 1 2 3 4 5
Mon 15 Mar	**Wed 24 Mar**	**Wed 31 Mar**	**Tues 6 April**
Emotion 1 2 3 4 5 Physical 1 2 3 4 5 Energy 1 2 3 4 5 Mental 1 2 3 4 5 Head/Heart 1 2 3 4 5	Emotion 1 2 3 4 5 Physical 1 2 3 4 5 Energy 1 2 3 4 5 Mental 1 2 3 4 5 Head/Heart 1 2 3 4 5	Emotion 1 2 3 4 5 Physical 1 2 3 4 5 Energy 1 2 3 4 5 Mental 1 2 3 4 5 Head/Heart 1 2 3 4 5	Emotion 1 2 3 4 5 Physical 1 2 3 4 5 Energy 1 2 3 4 5 Mental 1 2 3 4 5 Head/Heart 1 2 3 4 5
Tues 16 Mar	**Thurs 25 Mar**	**Thurs 1 April**	**Wed 7 April**
Emotion 1 2 3 4 5 Physical 1 2 3 4 5 Energy 1 2 3 4 5 Mental 1 2 3 4 5 Head/Heart 1 2 3 4 5	Emotion 1 2 3 4 5 Physical 1 2 3 4 5 Energy 1 2 3 4 5 Mental 1 2 3 4 5 Head/Heart 1 2 3 4 5	Emotion 1 2 3 4 5 Physical 1 2 3 4 5 Energy 1 2 3 4 5 Mental 1 2 3 4 5 Head/Heart 1 2 3 4 5	Emotion 1 2 3 4 5 Physical 1 2 3 4 5 Energy 1 2 3 4 5 Mental 1 2 3 4 5 Head/Heart 1 2 3 4 5
Wed 17 Mar	**Fri 26 Mar**	**Fri 2 April**	**Thurs 8 April**
Emotion 1 2 3 4 5 Physical 1 2 3 4 5 Energy 1 2 3 4 5 Mental 1 2 3 4 5 Head/Heart 1 2 3 4 5	Emotion 1 2 3 4 5 Physical 1 2 3 4 5 Energy 1 2 3 4 5 Mental 1 2 3 4 5 Head/Heart 1 2 3 4 5	Emotion 1 2 3 4 5 Physical 1 2 3 4 5 Energy 1 2 3 4 5 Mental 1 2 3 4 5 Head/Heart 1 2 3 4 5	Emotion 1 2 3 4 5 Physical 1 2 3 4 5 Energy 1 2 3 4 5 Mental 1 2 3 4 5 Head/Heart 1 2 3 4 5
Thurs 18 Mar	**Sat 27 Mar**	**Sat 3 April**	**Fri 9 April**
Emotion 1 2 3 4 5 Physical 1 2 3 4 5 Energy 1 2 3 4 5 Mental 1 2 3 4 5 Head/Heart 1 2 3 4 5	Emotion 1 2 3 4 5 Physical 1 2 3 4 5 Energy 1 2 3 4 5 Mental 1 2 3 4 5 Head/Heart 1 2 3 4 5	Emotion 1 2 3 4 5 Physical 1 2 3 4 5 Energy 1 2 3 4 5 Mental 1 2 3 4 5 Head/Heart 1 2 3 4 5	Emotion 1 2 3 4 5 Physical 1 2 3 4 5 Energy 1 2 3 4 5 Mental 1 2 3 4 5 Head/Heart 1 2 3 4 5
Fri 19 Mar	**Sun 28 Mar**		**Sat 10 April**
Emotion 1 2 3 4 5 Physical 1 2 3 4 5 Energy 1 2 3 4 5 Mental 1 2 3 4 5 Head/Heart 1 2 3 4 5	Emotion 1 2 3 4 5 Physical 1 2 3 4 5 Energy 1 2 3 4 5 Mental 1 2 3 4 5 Head/Heart 1 2 3 4 5		Emotion 1 2 3 4 5 Physical 1 2 3 4 5 Energy 1 2 3 4 5 Mental 1 2 3 4 5 Head/Heart 1 2 3 4 5
Sat 20 & Sun 21 Mar			**Sun 11 April**
Emotion 1 2 3 4 5 Physical 1 2 3 4 5 Energy 1 2 3 4 5 Mental 1 2 3 4 5 Head/Heart 1 2 3 4 5			Emotion 1 2 3 4 5 Physical 1 2 3 4 5 Energy 1 2 3 4 5 Mental 1 2 3 4 5 Head/Heart 1 2 3 4 5

Cycle 3

New Moon	First Quarter Moon	Full Moon	Last Quarter Moon
Mon 12 April Emotion 1 2 3 4 5 Physical 1 2 3 4 5 Energy 1 2 3 4 5 Mental 1 2 3 4 5 Head/Heart 1 2 3 4 5	**Tues 20 April** Emotion 1 2 3 4 5 Physical 1 2 3 4 5 Energy 1 2 3 4 5 Mental 1 2 3 4 5 Head/Heart 1 2 3 4 5	**Tues 27 April** Emotion 1 2 3 4 5 Physical 1 2 3 4 5 Energy 1 2 3 4 5 Mental 1 2 3 4 5 Head/Heart 1 2 3 4 5	**Tues 4 May** Emotion 1 2 3 4 5 Physical 1 2 3 4 5 Energy 1 2 3 4 5 Mental 1 2 3 4 5 Head/Heart 1 2 3 4 5
Tues 13 April Emotion 1 2 3 4 5 Physical 1 2 3 4 5 Energy 1 2 3 4 5 Mental 1 2 3 4 5 Head/Heart 1 2 3 4 5	**Wed 21 April** Emotion 1 2 3 4 5 Physical 1 2 3 4 5 Energy 1 2 3 4 5 Mental 1 2 3 4 5 Head/Heart 1 2 3 4 5	**Wed 28 April** Emotion 1 2 3 4 5 Physical 1 2 3 4 5 Energy 1 2 3 4 5 Mental 1 2 3 4 5 Head/Heart 1 2 3 4 5	**Wed 5 May** Emotion 1 2 3 4 5 Physical 1 2 3 4 5 Energy 1 2 3 4 5 Mental 1 2 3 4 5 Head/Heart 1 2 3 4 5
Wed 14 April Emotion 1 2 3 4 5 Physical 1 2 3 4 5 Energy 1 2 3 4 5 Mental 1 2 3 4 5 Head/Heart 1 2 3 4 5	**Thurs 22 April** Emotion 1 2 3 4 5 Physical 1 2 3 4 5 Energy 1 2 3 4 5 Mental 1 2 3 4 5 Head/Heart 1 2 3 4 5	**Thurs 29 April** Emotion 1 2 3 4 5 Physical 1 2 3 4 5 Energy 1 2 3 4 5 Mental 1 2 3 4 5 Head/Heart 1 2 3 4 5	**Thurs 6 May** Emotion 1 2 3 4 5 Physical 1 2 3 4 5 Energy 1 2 3 4 5 Mental 1 2 3 4 5 Head/Heart 1 2 3 4 5
Thurs 15 April Emotion 1 2 3 4 5 Physical 1 2 3 4 5 Energy 1 2 3 4 5 Mental 1 2 3 4 5 Head/Heart 1 2 3 4 5	**Fri 23 April** Emotion 1 2 3 4 5 Physical 1 2 3 4 5 Energy 1 2 3 4 5 Mental 1 2 3 4 5 Head/Heart 1 2 3 4 5	**Fri 30 April** Emotion 1 2 3 4 5 Physical 1 2 3 4 5 Energy 1 2 3 4 5 Mental 1 2 3 4 5 Head/Heart 1 2 3 4 5	**Fri 7 May** Emotion 1 2 3 4 5 Physical 1 2 3 4 5 Energy 1 2 3 4 5 Mental 1 2 3 4 5 Head/Heart 1 2 3 4 5
Fri 16 April Emotion 1 2 3 4 5 Physical 1 2 3 4 5 Energy 1 2 3 4 5 Mental 1 2 3 4 5 Head/Heart 1 2 3 4 5	**Sat 24 April** Emotion 1 2 3 4 5 Physical 1 2 3 4 5 Energy 1 2 3 4 5 Mental 1 2 3 4 5 Head/Heart 1 2 3 4 5	**Sat 1 May** Emotion 1 2 3 4 5 Physical 1 2 3 4 5 Energy 1 2 3 4 5 Mental 1 2 3 4 5 Head/Heart 1 2 3 4 5	**Sat 8 May** Emotion 1 2 3 4 5 Physical 1 2 3 4 5 Energy 1 2 3 4 5 Mental 1 2 3 4 5 Head/Heart 1 2 3 4 5
Sat 17 April Emotion 1 2 3 4 5 Physical 1 2 3 4 5 Energy 1 2 3 4 5 Mental 1 2 3 4 5 Head/Heart 1 2 3 4 5	**Sun 25 April** Emotion 1 2 3 4 5 Physical 1 2 3 4 5 Energy 1 2 3 4 5 Mental 1 2 3 4 5 Head/Heart 1 2 3 4 5	**Sun 2 May** Emotion 1 2 3 4 5 Physical 1 2 3 4 5 Energy 1 2 3 4 5 Mental 1 2 3 4 5 Head/Heart 1 2 3 4 5	**Sun 9 May** Emotion 1 2 3 4 5 Physical 1 2 3 4 5 Energy 1 2 3 4 5 Mental 1 2 3 4 5 Head/Heart 1 2 3 4 5
Sun 18 April Emotion 1 2 3 4 5 Physical 1 2 3 4 5 Energy 1 2 3 4 5 Mental 1 2 3 4 5 Head/Heart 1 2 3 4 5	**Mon 26 April** Emotion 1 2 3 4 5 Physical 1 2 3 4 5 Energy 1 2 3 4 5 Mental 1 2 3 4 5 Head/Heart 1 2 3 4 5	**Mon 3 May** Emotion 1 2 3 4 5 Physical 1 2 3 4 5 Energy 1 2 3 4 5 Mental 1 2 3 4 5 Head/Heart 1 2 3 4 5	**Mon 10 May** Emotion 1 2 3 4 5 Physical 1 2 3 4 5 Energy 1 2 3 4 5 Mental 1 2 3 4 5 Head/Heart 1 2 3 4 5
Mon 19 April Emotion 1 2 3 4 5 Physical 1 2 3 4 5 Energy 1 2 3 4 5 Mental 1 2 3 4 5 Head/Heart 1 2 3 4 5			**Tues 11 May** Emotion 1 2 3 4 5 Physical 1 2 3 4 5 Energy 1 2 3 4 5 Mental 1 2 3 4 5 Head/Heart 1 2 3 4 5

Cycle 4

New Moon	First Quarter Moon	Full Moon	Last Quarter Moon
Wed 12 May	Thurs 20 May	Wed 26 May	Wed 2 June
Emotion 1 2 3 4 5 Physical 1 2 3 4 5 Energy 1 2 3 4 5 Mental 1 2 3 4 5 Head/Heart 1 2 3 4 5	Emotion 1 2 3 4 5 Physical 1 2 3 4 5 Energy 1 2 3 4 5 Mental 1 2 3 4 5 Head/Heart 1 2 3 4 5	Emotion 1 2 3 4 5 Physical 1 2 3 4 5 Energy 1 2 3 4 5 Mental 1 2 3 4 5 Head/Heart 1 2 3 4 5	Emotion 1 2 3 4 5 Physical 1 2 3 4 5 Energy 1 2 3 4 5 Mental 1 2 3 4 5 Head/Heart 1 2 3 4 5
Thurs 13 May	Fri 21 May	Thurs 27 May	Thurs 3 June
Emotion 1 2 3 4 5 Physical 1 2 3 4 5 Energy 1 2 3 4 5 Mental 1 2 3 4 5 Head/Heart 1 2 3 4 5	Emotion 1 2 3 4 5 Physical 1 2 3 4 5 Energy 1 2 3 4 5 Mental 1 2 3 4 5 Head/Heart 1 2 3 4 5	Emotion 1 2 3 4 5 Physical 1 2 3 4 5 Energy 1 2 3 4 5 Mental 1 2 3 4 5 Head/Heart 1 2 3 4 5	Emotion 1 2 3 4 5 Physical 1 2 3 4 5 Energy 1 2 3 4 5 Mental 1 2 3 4 5 Head/Heart 1 2 3 4 5
Fri 14 May	Sat 22 May	Fri 28 May	Fri 4 June
Emotion 1 2 3 4 5 Physical 1 2 3 4 5 Energy 1 2 3 4 5 Mental 1 2 3 4 5 Head/Heart 1 2 3 4 5	Emotion 1 2 3 4 5 Physical 1 2 3 4 5 Energy 1 2 3 4 5 Mental 1 2 3 4 5 Head/Heart 1 2 3 4 5	Emotion 1 2 3 4 5 Physical 1 2 3 4 5 Energy 1 2 3 4 5 Mental 1 2 3 4 5 Head/Heart 1 2 3 4 5	Emotion 1 2 3 4 5 Physical 1 2 3 4 5 Energy 1 2 3 4 5 Mental 1 2 3 4 5 Head/Heart 1 2 3 4 5
Sat 15 May	Sun 23 May	Sat 29 May	Sat 5 June
Emotion 1 2 3 4 5 Physical 1 2 3 4 5 Energy 1 2 3 4 5 Mental 1 2 3 4 5 Head/Heart 1 2 3 4 5	Emotion 1 2 3 4 5 Physical 1 2 3 4 5 Energy 1 2 3 4 5 Mental 1 2 3 4 5 Head/Heart 1 2 3 4 5	Emotion 1 2 3 4 5 Physical 1 2 3 4 5 Energy 1 2 3 4 5 Mental 1 2 3 4 5 Head/Heart 1 2 3 4 5	Emotion 1 2 3 4 5 Physical 1 2 3 4 5 Energy 1 2 3 4 5 Mental 1 2 3 4 5 Head/Heart 1 2 3 4 5
Sun 16 May	Mon 24 May	Sun 30 May	Sun 6 June
Emotion 1 2 3 4 5 Physical 1 2 3 4 5 Energy 1 2 3 4 5 Mental 1 2 3 4 5 Head/Heart 1 2 3 4 5	Emotion 1 2 3 4 5 Physical 1 2 3 4 5 Energy 1 2 3 4 5 Mental 1 2 3 4 5 Head/Heart 1 2 3 4 5	Emotion 1 2 3 4 5 Physical 1 2 3 4 5 Energy 1 2 3 4 5 Mental 1 2 3 4 5 Head/Heart 1 2 3 4 5	Emotion 1 2 3 4 5 Physical 1 2 3 4 5 Energy 1 2 3 4 5 Mental 1 2 3 4 5 Head/Heart 1 2 3 4 5
Mon 17 May	Tues 25 May	Mon 31 May	Mon 7 June
Emotion 1 2 3 4 5 Physical 1 2 3 4 5 Energy 1 2 3 4 5 Mental 1 2 3 4 5 Head/Heart 1 2 3 4 5	Emotion 1 2 3 4 5 Physical 1 2 3 4 5 Energy 1 2 3 4 5 Mental 1 2 3 4 5 Head/Heart 1 2 3 4 5	Emotion 1 2 3 4 5 Physical 1 2 3 4 5 Energy 1 2 3 4 5 Mental 1 2 3 4 5 Head/Heart 1 2 3 4 5	Emotion 1 2 3 4 5 Physical 1 2 3 4 5 Energy 1 2 3 4 5 Mental 1 2 3 4 5 Head/Heart 1 2 3 4 5
Tues 18 May		Tues 1 June	Tues 8 June
Emotion 1 2 3 4 5 Physical 1 2 3 4 5 Energy 1 2 3 4 5 Mental 1 2 3 4 5 Head/Heart 1 2 3 4 5		Emotion 1 2 3 4 5 Physical 1 2 3 4 5 Energy 1 2 3 4 5 Mental 1 2 3 4 5 Head/Heart 1 2 3 4 5	Emotion 1 2 3 4 5 Physical 1 2 3 4 5 Energy 1 2 3 4 5 Mental 1 2 3 4 5 Head/Heart 1 2 3 4 5
Wed 19 May			Wed 9 June
Emotion 1 2 3 4 5 Physical 1 2 3 4 5 Energy 1 2 3 4 5 Mental 1 2 3 4 5 Head/Heart 1 2 3 4 5			Emotion 1 2 3 4 5 Physical 1 2 3 4 5 Energy 1 2 3 4 5 Mental 1 2 3 4 5 Head/Heart 1 2 3 4 5

Cycle 5

New Moon	First Quarter Moon	Full Moon	Last Quarter Moon
Thurs 10 June	**Fri 18 June**	**Fri 25 June**	**Fri 2 July**
Emotion 1 2 3 4 5	Emotion 1 2 3 4 5	Emotion 1 2 3 4 5	Emotion 1 2 3 4 5
Physical 1 2 3 4 5	Physical 1 2 3 4 5	Physical 1 2 3 4 5	Physical 1 2 3 4 5
Energy 1 2 3 4 5	Energy 1 2 3 4 5	Energy 1 2 3 4 5	Energy 1 2 3 4 5
Mental 1 2 3 4 5	Mental 1 2 3 4 5	Mental 1 2 3 4 5	Mental 1 2 3 4 5
Head/Heart 1 2 3 4 5	Head/Heart 1 2 3 4 5	Head/Heart 1 2 3 4 5	Head/Heart 1 2 3 4 5
Fri 11 June	**Sat 19 June**	**Sat 26 June**	**Sat 3 July**
Emotion 1 2 3 4 5	Emotion 1 2 3 4 5	Emotion 1 2 3 4 5	Emotion 1 2 3 4 5
Physical 1 2 3 4 5	Physical 1 2 3 4 5	Physical 1 2 3 4 5	Physical 1 2 3 4 5
Energy 1 2 3 4 5	Energy 1 2 3 4 5	Energy 1 2 3 4 5	Energy 1 2 3 4 5
Mental 1 2 3 4 5	Mental 1 2 3 4 5	Mental 1 2 3 4 5	Mental 1 2 3 4 5
Head/Heart 1 2 3 4 5	Head/Heart 1 2 3 4 5	Head/Heart 1 2 3 4 5	Head/Heart 1 2 3 4 5
Sat 12 June	**Sun 20 June**	**Sun 27 June**	**Sun 4 July**
Emotion 1 2 3 4 5	Emotion 1 2 3 4 5	Emotion 1 2 3 4 5	Emotion 1 2 3 4 5
Physical 1 2 3 4 5	Physical 1 2 3 4 5	Physical 1 2 3 4 5	Physical 1 2 3 4 5
Energy 1 2 3 4 5	Energy 1 2 3 4 5	Energy 1 2 3 4 5	Energy 1 2 3 4 5
Mental 1 2 3 4 5	Mental 1 2 3 4 5	Mental 1 2 3 4 5	Mental 1 2 3 4 5
Head/Heart 1 2 3 4 5	Head/Heart 1 2 3 4 5	Head/Heart 1 2 3 4 5	Head/Heart 1 2 3 4 5
Sun 13 June	**Mon 21 June**	**Mon 28 June**	**Mon 5 July**
Emotion 1 2 3 4 5	Emotion 1 2 3 4 5	Emotion 1 2 3 4 5	Emotion 1 2 3 4 5
Physical 1 2 3 4 5	Physical 1 2 3 4 5	Physical 1 2 3 4 5	Physical 1 2 3 4 5
Energy 1 2 3 4 5	Energy 1 2 3 4 5	Energy 1 2 3 4 5	Energy 1 2 3 4 5
Mental 1 2 3 4 5	Mental 1 2 3 4 5	Mental 1 2 3 4 5	Mental 1 2 3 4 5
Head/Heart 1 2 3 4 5	Head/Heart 1 2 3 4 5	Head/Heart 1 2 3 4 5	Head/Heart 1 2 3 4 5
Mon 14 June	**Tues 22 June**	**Tues 29 June**	**Tues 6 July**
Emotion 1 2 3 4 5	Emotion 1 2 3 4 5	Emotion 1 2 3 4 5	Emotion 1 2 3 4 5
Physical 1 2 3 4 5	Physical 1 2 3 4 5	Physical 1 2 3 4 5	Physical 1 2 3 4 5
Energy 1 2 3 4 5	Energy 1 2 3 4 5	Energy 1 2 3 4 5	Energy 1 2 3 4 5
Mental 1 2 3 4 5	Mental 1 2 3 4 5	Mental 1 2 3 4 5	Mental 1 2 3 4 5
Head/Heart 1 2 3 4 5	Head/Heart 1 2 3 4 5	Head/Heart 1 2 3 4 5	Head/Heart 1 2 3 4 5
Tues 15 June	**Wed 23 June**	**Wed 30 June**	**Wed 7 July**
Emotion 1 2 3 4 5	Emotion 1 2 3 4 5	Emotion 1 2 3 4 5	Emotion 1 2 3 4 5
Physical 1 2 3 4 5	Physical 1 2 3 4 5	Physical 1 2 3 4 5	Physical 1 2 3 4 5
Energy 1 2 3 4 5	Energy 1 2 3 4 5	Energy 1 2 3 4 5	Energy 1 2 3 4 5
Mental 1 2 3 4 5	Mental 1 2 3 4 5	Mental 1 2 3 4 5	Mental 1 2 3 4 5
Head/Heart 1 2 3 4 5	Head/Heart 1 2 3 4 5	Head/Heart 1 2 3 4 5	Head/Heart 1 2 3 4 5
Wed 16 June	**Thurs 24 June**	**Thurs 1 July**	**Thurs 8 July**
Emotion 1 2 3 4 5	Emotion 1 2 3 4 5	Emotion 1 2 3 4 5	Emotion 1 2 3 4 5
Physical 1 2 3 4 5	Physical 1 2 3 4 5	Physical 1 2 3 4 5	Physical 1 2 3 4 5
Energy 1 2 3 4 5	Energy 1 2 3 4 5	Energy 1 2 3 4 5	Energy 1 2 3 4 5
Mental 1 2 3 4 5	Mental 1 2 3 4 5	Mental 1 2 3 4 5	Mental 1 2 3 4 5
Head/Heart 1 2 3 4 5	Head/Heart 1 2 3 4 5	Head/Heart 1 2 3 4 5	Head/Heart 1 2 3 4 5
Thurs 17 June			**Fri 9 July**
Emotion 1 2 3 4 5			Emotion 1 2 3 4 5
Physical 1 2 3 4 5			Physical 1 2 3 4 5
Energy 1 2 3 4 5			Energy 1 2 3 4 5
Mental 1 2 3 4 5			Mental 1 2 3 4 5
Head/Heart 1 2 3 4 5			Head/Heart 1 2 3 4 5

Cycle 6

New Moon	First Quarter Moon	Full Moon	Last Quarter Moon
Sat 10 July	**Sat 17 July**	**Sat 24 July**	**Sat 31 July**
Emotion 1 2 3 4 5 Physical 1 2 3 4 5 Energy 1 2 3 4 5 Mental 1 2 3 4 5 Head/Heart 1 2 3 4 5	Emotion 1 2 3 4 5 Physical 1 2 3 4 5 Energy 1 2 3 4 5 Mental 1 2 3 4 5 Head/Heart 1 2 3 4 5	Emotion 1 2 3 4 5 Physical 1 2 3 4 5 Energy 1 2 3 4 5 Mental 1 2 3 4 5 Head/Heart 1 2 3 4 5	Emotion 1 2 3 4 5 Physical 1 2 3 4 5 Energy 1 2 3 4 5 Mental 1 2 3 4 5 Head/Heart 1 2 3 4 5
Sun 11 July	**Sun 18 July**	**Sun 25 July**	**Sun 1 August**
Emotion 1 2 3 4 5 Physical 1 2 3 4 5 Energy 1 2 3 4 5 Mental 1 2 3 4 5 Head/Heart 1 2 3 4 5	Emotion 1 2 3 4 5 Physical 1 2 3 4 5 Energy 1 2 3 4 5 Mental 1 2 3 4 5 Head/Heart 1 2 3 4 5	Emotion 1 2 3 4 5 Physical 1 2 3 4 5 Energy 1 2 3 4 5 Mental 1 2 3 4 5 Head/Heart 1 2 3 4 5	Emotion 1 2 3 4 5 Physical 1 2 3 4 5 Energy 1 2 3 4 5 Mental 1 2 3 4 5 Head/Heart 1 2 3 4 5
Mon 12 July	**Mon 19 July**	**Mon 26 July**	**Mon 2 August**
Emotion 1 2 3 4 5 Physical 1 2 3 4 5 Energy 1 2 3 4 5 Mental 1 2 3 4 5 Head/Heart 1 2 3 4 5	Emotion 1 2 3 4 5 Physical 1 2 3 4 5 Energy 1 2 3 4 5 Mental 1 2 3 4 5 Head/Heart 1 2 3 4 5	Emotion 1 2 3 4 5 Physical 1 2 3 4 5 Energy 1 2 3 4 5 Mental 1 2 3 4 5 Head/Heart 1 2 3 4 5	Emotion 1 2 3 4 5 Physical 1 2 3 4 5 Energy 1 2 3 4 5 Mental 1 2 3 4 5 Head/Heart 1 2 3 4 5
Tues 13 July	**Tues 20 July**	**Tues 27 July**	**Tues 3 August**
Emotion 1 2 3 4 5 Physical 1 2 3 4 5 Energy 1 2 3 4 5 Mental 1 2 3 4 5 Head/Heart 1 2 3 4 5	Emotion 1 2 3 4 5 Physical 1 2 3 4 5 Energy 1 2 3 4 5 Mental 1 2 3 4 5 Head/Heart 1 2 3 4 5	Emotion 1 2 3 4 5 Physical 1 2 3 4 5 Energy 1 2 3 4 5 Mental 1 2 3 4 5 Head/Heart 1 2 3 4 5	Emotion 1 2 3 4 5 Physical 1 2 3 4 5 Energy 1 2 3 4 5 Mental 1 2 3 4 5 Head/Heart 1 2 3 4 5
Wed 14 July	**Wed 21 July**	**Wed 28 July**	**Wed 4 August**
Emotion 1 2 3 4 5 Physical 1 2 3 4 5 Energy 1 2 3 4 5 Mental 1 2 3 4 5 Head/Heart 1 2 3 4 5	Emotion 1 2 3 4 5 Physical 1 2 3 4 5 Energy 1 2 3 4 5 Mental 1 2 3 4 5 Head/Heart 1 2 3 4 5	Emotion 1 2 3 4 5 Physical 1 2 3 4 5 Energy 1 2 3 4 5 Mental 1 2 3 4 5 Head/Heart 1 2 3 4 5	Emotion 1 2 3 4 5 Physical 1 2 3 4 5 Energy 1 2 3 4 5 Mental 1 2 3 4 5 Head/Heart 1 2 3 4 5
Thurs 15 July	**Thurs 23 July**	**Thurs 29 July**	**Thurs 5 August**
Emotion 1 2 3 4 5 Physical 1 2 3 4 5 Energy 1 2 3 4 5 Mental 1 2 3 4 5 Head/Heart 1 2 3 4 5	Emotion 1 2 3 4 5 Physical 1 2 3 4 5 Energy 1 2 3 4 5 Mental 1 2 3 4 5 Head/Heart 1 2 3 4 5	Emotion 1 2 3 4 5 Physical 1 2 3 4 5 Energy 1 2 3 4 5 Mental 1 2 3 4 5 Head/Heart 1 2 3 4 5	Emotion 1 2 3 4 5 Physical 1 2 3 4 5 Energy 1 2 3 4 5 Mental 1 2 3 4 5 Head/Heart 1 2 3 4 5
Fri 16 July		**Fri 30 July**	**Fri 6 August**
Emotion 1 2 3 4 5 Physical 1 2 3 4 5 Energy 1 2 3 4 5 Mental 1 2 3 4 5 Head/Heart 1 2 3 4 5		Emotion 1 2 3 4 5 Physical 1 2 3 4 5 Energy 1 2 3 4 5 Mental 1 2 3 4 5 Head/Heart 1 2 3 4 5	Emotion 1 2 3 4 5 Physical 1 2 3 4 5 Energy 1 2 3 4 5 Mental 1 2 3 4 5 Head/Heart 1 2 3 4 5
			Sat 7 August
			Emotion 1 2 3 4 5 Physical 1 2 3 4 5 Energy 1 2 3 4 5 Mental 1 2 3 4 5 Head/Heart 1 2 3 4 5

Cycle 7

New Moon	First Quarter Moon	Full Moon	Last Quarter Moon
Sun 8 August Emotion 1 2 3 4 5 Physical 1 2 3 4 5 Energy 1 2 3 4 5 Mental 1 2 3 4 5 Head/Heart 1 2 3 4 5	**Mon 16 August** Emotion 1 2 3 4 5 Physical 1 2 3 4 5 Energy 1 2 3 4 5 Mental 1 2 3 4 5 Head/Heart 1 2 3 4 5	**Sun 22 August** Emotion 1 2 3 4 5 Physical 1 2 3 4 5 Energy 1 2 3 4 5 Mental 1 2 3 4 5 Head/Heart 1 2 3 4 5	**Mon 30 August** Emotion 1 2 3 4 5 Physical 1 2 3 4 5 Energy 1 2 3 4 5 Mental 1 2 3 4 5 Head/Heart 1 2 3 4 5
Mon 9 August Emotion 1 2 3 4 5 Physical 1 2 3 4 5 Energy 1 2 3 4 5 Mental 1 2 3 4 5 Head/Heart 1 2 3 4 5	**Tues 17 August** Emotion 1 2 3 4 5 Physical 1 2 3 4 5 Energy 1 2 3 4 5 Mental 1 2 3 4 5 Head/Heart 1 2 3 4 5	**Mon 23 August** Emotion 1 2 3 4 5 Physical 1 2 3 4 5 Energy 1 2 3 4 5 Mental 1 2 3 4 5 Head/Heart 1 2 3 4 5	**Tues 31 August** Emotion 1 2 3 4 5 Physical 1 2 3 4 5 Energy 1 2 3 4 5 Mental 1 2 3 4 5 Head/Heart 1 2 3 4 5
Tues 10 August Emotion 1 2 3 4 5 Physical 1 2 3 4 5 Energy 1 2 3 4 5 Mental 1 2 3 4 5 Head/Heart 1 2 3 4 5	**Wed 18 August** Emotion 1 2 3 4 5 Physical 1 2 3 4 5 Energy 1 2 3 4 5 Mental 1 2 3 4 5 Head/Heart 1 2 3 4 5	**Tues 24 August** Emotion 1 2 3 4 5 Physical 1 2 3 4 5 Energy 1 2 3 4 5 Mental 1 2 3 4 5 Head/Heart 1 2 3 4 5	**Wed 1 September** Emotion 1 2 3 4 5 Physical 1 2 3 4 5 Energy 1 2 3 4 5 Mental 1 2 3 4 5 Head/Heart 1 2 3 4 5
Wed 11 August Emotion 1 2 3 4 5 Physical 1 2 3 4 5 Energy 1 2 3 4 5 Mental 1 2 3 4 5 Head/Heart 1 2 3 4 5	**Thurs 19 August** Emotion 1 2 3 4 5 Physical 1 2 3 4 5 Energy 1 2 3 4 5 Mental 1 2 3 4 5 Head/Heart 1 2 3 4 5	**Wed 25 August** Emotion 1 2 3 4 5 Physical 1 2 3 4 5 Energy 1 2 3 4 5 Mental 1 2 3 4 5 Head/Heart 1 2 3 4 5	**Thurs 2 September** Emotion 1 2 3 4 5 Physical 1 2 3 4 5 Energy 1 2 3 4 5 Mental 1 2 3 4 5 Head/Heart 1 2 3 4 5
Thurs 12 August Emotion 1 2 3 4 5 Physical 1 2 3 4 5 Energy 1 2 3 4 5 Mental 1 2 3 4 5 Head/Heart 1 2 3 4 5	**Fri 20 August** Emotion 1 2 3 4 5 Physical 1 2 3 4 5 Energy 1 2 3 4 5 Mental 1 2 3 4 5 Head/Heart 1 2 3 4 5	**Thurs 26 August** Emotion 1 2 3 4 5 Physical 1 2 3 4 5 Energy 1 2 3 4 5 Mental 1 2 3 4 5 Head/Heart 1 2 3 4 5	**Fri 3 September** Emotion 1 2 3 4 5 Physical 1 2 3 4 5 Energy 1 2 3 4 5 Mental 1 2 3 4 5 Head/Heart 1 2 3 4 5
Fri 13 August Emotion 1 2 3 4 5 Physical 1 2 3 4 5 Energy 1 2 3 4 5 Mental 1 2 3 4 5 Head/Heart 1 2 3 4 5	**Sat 21 August** Emotion 1 2 3 4 5 Physical 1 2 3 4 5 Energy 1 2 3 4 5 Mental 1 2 3 4 5 Head/Heart 1 2 3 4 5	**Fri 27 August** Emotion 1 2 3 4 5 Physical 1 2 3 4 5 Energy 1 2 3 4 5 Mental 1 2 3 4 5 Head/Heart 1 2 3 4 5	**Sat 4 September** Emotion 1 2 3 4 5 Physical 1 2 3 4 5 Energy 1 2 3 4 5 Mental 1 2 3 4 5 Head/Heart 1 2 3 4 5
Sat 14 August Emotion 1 2 3 4 5 Physical 1 2 3 4 5 Energy 1 2 3 4 5 Mental 1 2 3 4 5 Head/Heart 1 2 3 4 5		**Sat 28 August** Emotion 1 2 3 4 5 Physical 1 2 3 4 5 Energy 1 2 3 4 5 Mental 1 2 3 4 5 Head/Heart 1 2 3 4 5	**Sun 5 September** Emotion 1 2 3 4 5 Physical 1 2 3 4 5 Energy 1 2 3 4 5 Mental 1 2 3 4 5 Head/Heart 1 2 3 4 5
Sun 15 August Emotion 1 2 3 4 5 Physical 1 2 3 4 5 Energy 1 2 3 4 5 Mental 1 2 3 4 5 Head/Heart 1 2 3 4 5		**Sun 29 August** Emotion 1 2 3 4 5 Physical 1 2 3 4 5 Energy 1 2 3 4 5 Mental 1 2 3 4 5 Head/Heart 1 2 3 4 5	**Mon 6 September** Emotion 1 2 3 4 5 Physical 1 2 3 4 5 Energy 1 2 3 4 5 Mental 1 2 3 4 5 Head/Heart 1 2 3 4 5

Cycle 8

New Moon	First Quarter Moon	Full Moon	Last Quarter Moon
Tues 7 September Emotion 1 2 3 4 5 Physical 1 2 3 4 5 Energy 1 2 3 4 5 Mental 1 2 3 4 5 Head/Heart 1 2 3 4 5	**Tues 14 September** Emotion 1 2 3 4 5 Physical 1 2 3 4 5 Energy 1 2 3 4 5 Mental 1 2 3 4 5 Head/Heart 1 2 3 4 5	**Tues 21 September** Emotion 1 2 3 4 5 Physical 1 2 3 4 5 Energy 1 2 3 4 5 Mental 1 2 3 4 5 Head/Heart 1 2 3 4 5	**Wed 29 September** Emotion 1 2 3 4 5 Physical 1 2 3 4 5 Energy 1 2 3 4 5 Mental 1 2 3 4 5 Head/Heart 1 2 3 4 5
Wed 8 September Emotion 1 2 3 4 5 Physical 1 2 3 4 5 Energy 1 2 3 4 5 Mental 1 2 3 4 5 Head/Heart 1 2 3 4 5	**Wed 15 September** Emotion 1 2 3 4 5 Physical 1 2 3 4 5 Energy 1 2 3 4 5 Mental 1 2 3 4 5 Head/Heart 1 2 3 4 5	**Wed 22 September** Emotion 1 2 3 4 5 Physical 1 2 3 4 5 Energy 1 2 3 4 5 Mental 1 2 3 4 5 Head/Heart 1 2 3 4 5	**Thurs 30 September** Emotion 1 2 3 4 5 Physical 1 2 3 4 5 Energy 1 2 3 4 5 Mental 1 2 3 4 5 Head/Heart 1 2 3 4 5
Thurs 9 September Emotion 1 2 3 4 5 Physical 1 2 3 4 5 Energy 1 2 3 4 5 Mental 1 2 3 4 5 Head/Heart 1 2 3 4 5	**Thurs 16 September** Emotion 1 2 3 4 5 Physical 1 2 3 4 5 Energy 1 2 3 4 5 Mental 1 2 3 4 5 Head/Heart 1 2 3 4 5	**Thurs 23 September** Emotion 1 2 3 4 5 Physical 1 2 3 4 5 Energy 1 2 3 4 5 Mental 1 2 3 4 5 Head/Heart 1 2 3 4 5	**Fri 1 October** Emotion 1 2 3 4 5 Physical 1 2 3 4 5 Energy 1 2 3 4 5 Mental 1 2 3 4 5 Head/Heart 1 2 3 4 5
Fri 10 September Emotion 1 2 3 4 5 Physical 1 2 3 4 5 Energy 1 2 3 4 5 Mental 1 2 3 4 5 Head/Heart 1 2 3 4 5	**Fri 17 September** Emotion 1 2 3 4 5 Physical 1 2 3 4 5 Energy 1 2 3 4 5 Mental 1 2 3 4 5 Head/Heart 1 2 3 4 5	**Fri 24 September** Emotion 1 2 3 4 5 Physical 1 2 3 4 5 Energy 1 2 3 4 5 Mental 1 2 3 4 5 Head/Heart 1 2 3 4 5	**Sat 2 October** Emotion 1 2 3 4 5 Physical 1 2 3 4 5 Energy 1 2 3 4 5 Mental 1 2 3 4 5 Head/Heart 1 2 3 4 5
Sat 11 September Emotion 1 2 3 4 5 Physical 1 2 3 4 5 Energy 1 2 3 4 5 Mental 1 2 3 4 5 Head/Heart 1 2 3 4 5	**Sat 18 September** Emotion 1 2 3 4 5 Physical 1 2 3 4 5 Energy 1 2 3 4 5 Mental 1 2 3 4 5 Head/Heart 1 2 3 4 5	**Sat 25 September** Emotion 1 2 3 4 5 Physical 1 2 3 4 5 Energy 1 2 3 4 5 Mental 1 2 3 4 5 Head/Heart 1 2 3 4 5	**Sun 3 October** Emotion 1 2 3 4 5 Physical 1 2 3 4 5 Energy 1 2 3 4 5 Mental 1 2 3 4 5 Head/Heart 1 2 3 4 5
Sun 12 September Emotion 1 2 3 4 5 Physical 1 2 3 4 5 Energy 1 2 3 4 5 Mental 1 2 3 4 5 Head/Heart 1 2 3 4 5	**Sun 19 September** Emotion 1 2 3 4 5 Physical 1 2 3 4 5 Energy 1 2 3 4 5 Mental 1 2 3 4 5 Head/Heart 1 2 3 4 5	**Sun 26 September** Emotion 1 2 3 4 5 Physical 1 2 3 4 5 Energy 1 2 3 4 5 Mental 1 2 3 4 5 Head/Heart 1 2 3 4 5	**Mon 4 October** Emotion 1 2 3 4 5 Physical 1 2 3 4 5 Energy 1 2 3 4 5 Mental 1 2 3 4 5 Head/Heart 1 2 3 4 5
Mon 13 September Emotion 1 2 3 4 5 Physical 1 2 3 4 5 Energy 1 2 3 4 5 Mental 1 2 3 4 5 Head/Heart 1 2 3 4 5	**Mon 20 September** Emotion 1 2 3 4 5 Physical 1 2 3 4 5 Energy 1 2 3 4 5 Mental 1 2 3 4 5 Head/Heart 1 2 3 4 5	**Mon 27 September** Emotion 1 2 3 4 5 Physical 1 2 3 4 5 Energy 1 2 3 4 5 Mental 1 2 3 4 5 Head/Heart 1 2 3 4 5	**Tues 5 October** Emotion 1 2 3 4 5 Physical 1 2 3 4 5 Energy 1 2 3 4 5 Mental 1 2 3 4 5 Head/Heart 1 2 3 4 5
		Tues 28 September Emotion 1 2 3 4 5 Physical 1 2 3 4 5 Energy 1 2 3 4 5 Mental 1 2 3 4 5 Head/Heart 1 2 3 4 5	

Cycle 9

New Moon	First Quarter Moon	Full Moon	Last Quarter Moon
Wed 6 October	Wed 13 October	Thurs 21 October	Fri 29 October
Emotion 1 2 3 4 5 Physical 1 2 3 4 5 Energy 1 2 3 4 5 Mental 1 2 3 4 5 Head/Heart 1 2 3 4 5	Emotion 1 2 3 4 5 Physical 1 2 3 4 5 Energy 1 2 3 4 5 Mental 1 2 3 4 5 Head/Heart 1 2 3 4 5	Emotion 1 2 3 4 5 Physical 1 2 3 4 5 Energy 1 2 3 4 5 Mental 1 2 3 4 5 Head/Heart 1 2 3 4 5	Emotion 1 2 3 4 5 Physical 1 2 3 4 5 Energy 1 2 3 4 5 Mental 1 2 3 4 5 Head/Heart 1 2 3 4 5
Thurs 7 October	Thurs 14 October	Fri 22 October	Sat 30 October
Emotion 1 2 3 4 5 Physical 1 2 3 4 5 Energy 1 2 3 4 5 Mental 1 2 3 4 5 Head/Heart 1 2 3 4 5	Emotion 1 2 3 4 5 Physical 1 2 3 4 5 Energy 1 2 3 4 5 Mental 1 2 3 4 5 Head/Heart 1 2 3 4 5	Emotion 1 2 3 4 5 Physical 1 2 3 4 5 Energy 1 2 3 4 5 Mental 1 2 3 4 5 Head/Heart 1 2 3 4 5	Emotion 1 2 3 4 5 Physical 1 2 3 4 5 Energy 1 2 3 4 5 Mental 1 2 3 4 5 Head/Heart 1 2 3 4 5
Fri 8 October	Fri 15 October	Sat 23 October	Sun 31 October
Emotion 1 2 3 4 5 Physical 1 2 3 4 5 Energy 1 2 3 4 5 Mental 1 2 3 4 5 Head/Heart 1 2 3 4 5	Emotion 1 2 3 4 5 Physical 1 2 3 4 5 Energy 1 2 3 4 5 Mental 1 2 3 4 5 Head/Heart 1 2 3 4 5	Emotion 1 2 3 4 5 Physical 1 2 3 4 5 Energy 1 2 3 4 5 Mental 1 2 3 4 5 Head/Heart 1 2 3 4 5	Emotion 1 2 3 4 5 Physical 1 2 3 4 5 Energy 1 2 3 4 5 Mental 1 2 3 4 5 Head/Heart 1 2 3 4 5
Sat 9 October	Sat 16 October	Sun 24 October	Mon 1 November
Emotion 1 2 3 4 5 Physical 1 2 3 4 5 Energy 1 2 3 4 5 Mental 1 2 3 4 5 Head/Heart 1 2 3 4 5	Emotion 1 2 3 4 5 Physical 1 2 3 4 5 Energy 1 2 3 4 5 Mental 1 2 3 4 5 Head/Heart 1 2 3 4 5	Emotion 1 2 3 4 5 Physical 1 2 3 4 5 Energy 1 2 3 4 5 Mental 1 2 3 4 5 Head/Heart 1 2 3 4 5	Emotion 1 2 3 4 5 Physical 1 2 3 4 5 Energy 1 2 3 4 5 Mental 1 2 3 4 5 Head/Heart 1 2 3 4 5
Sun 10 October	Sun 17 October	Mon 25 October	Tues 2 November
Emotion 1 2 3 4 5 Physical 1 2 3 4 5 Energy 1 2 3 4 5 Mental 1 2 3 4 5 Head/Heart 1 2 3 4 5	Emotion 1 2 3 4 5 Physical 1 2 3 4 5 Energy 1 2 3 4 5 Mental 1 2 3 4 5 Head/Heart 1 2 3 4 5	Emotion 1 2 3 4 5 Physical 1 2 3 4 5 Energy 1 2 3 4 5 Mental 1 2 3 4 5 Head/Heart 1 2 3 4 5	Emotion 1 2 3 4 5 Physical 1 2 3 4 5 Energy 1 2 3 4 5 Mental 1 2 3 4 5 Head/Heart 1 2 3 4 5
Mon 11 October	Mon 18 October	Tues 26 October	Wed 3 November
Emotion 1 2 3 4 5 Physical 1 2 3 4 5 Energy 1 2 3 4 5 Mental 1 2 3 4 5 Head/Heart 1 2 3 4 5	Emotion 1 2 3 4 5 Physical 1 2 3 4 5 Energy 1 2 3 4 5 Mental 1 2 3 4 5 Head/Heart 1 2 3 4 5	Emotion 1 2 3 4 5 Physical 1 2 3 4 5 Energy 1 2 3 4 5 Mental 1 2 3 4 5 Head/Heart 1 2 3 4 5	Emotion 1 2 3 4 5 Physical 1 2 3 4 5 Energy 1 2 3 4 5 Mental 1 2 3 4 5 Head/Heart 1 2 3 4 5
Tues 12 October	Tues 19 October	Wed 27 October	Thurs 4 November
Emotion 1 2 3 4 5 Physical 1 2 3 4 5 Energy 1 2 3 4 5 Mental 1 2 3 4 5 Head/Heart 1 2 3 4 5	Emotion 1 2 3 4 5 Physical 1 2 3 4 5 Energy 1 2 3 4 5 Mental 1 2 3 4 5 Head/Heart 1 2 3 4 5	Emotion 1 2 3 4 5 Physical 1 2 3 4 5 Energy 1 2 3 4 5 Mental 1 2 3 4 5 Head/Heart 1 2 3 4 5	Emotion 1 2 3 4 5 Physical 1 2 3 4 5 Energy 1 2 3 4 5 Mental 1 2 3 4 5 Head/Heart 1 2 3 4 5
	Wed 20 October	Thurs 28 October	
	Emotion 1 2 3 4 5 Physical 1 2 3 4 5 Energy 1 2 3 4 5 Mental 1 2 3 4 5 Head/Heart 1 2 3 4 5	Emotion 1 2 3 4 5 Physical 1 2 3 4 5 Energy 1 2 3 4 5 Mental 1 2 3 4 5 Head/Heart 1 2 3 4 5	

Cycle 10

New Moon	First Quarter Moon	Full Moon	Last Quarter Moon
Fri 5 November Emotion 1 2 3 4 5 Physical 1 2 3 4 5 Energy 1 2 3 4 5 Mental 1 2 3 4 5 Head/Heart 1 2 3 4 5	**Thurs 11 November** Emotion 1 2 3 4 5 Physical 1 2 3 4 5 Energy 1 2 3 4 5 Mental 1 2 3 4 5 Head/Heart 1 2 3 4 5	**Fri 19 November** Emotion 1 2 3 4 5 Physical 1 2 3 4 5 Energy 1 2 3 4 5 Mental 1 2 3 4 5 Head/Heart 1 2 3 4 5	**Sat 27 November** Emotion 1 2 3 4 5 Physical 1 2 3 4 5 Energy 1 2 3 4 5 Mental 1 2 3 4 5 Head/Heart 1 2 3 4 5
Sat 6 November Emotion 1 2 3 4 5 Physical 1 2 3 4 5 Energy 1 2 3 4 5 Mental 1 2 3 4 5 Head/Heart 1 2 3 4 5	**Fri 12 November** Emotion 1 2 3 4 5 Physical 1 2 3 4 5 Energy 1 2 3 4 5 Mental 1 2 3 4 5 Head/Heart 1 2 3 4 5	**Sat 20 November** Emotion 1 2 3 4 5 Physical 1 2 3 4 5 Energy 1 2 3 4 5 Mental 1 2 3 4 5 Head/Heart 1 2 3 4 5	**Sun 28 November** Emotion 1 2 3 4 5 Physical 1 2 3 4 5 Energy 1 2 3 4 5 Mental 1 2 3 4 5 Head/Heart 1 2 3 4 5
Sun 7 November Emotion 1 2 3 4 5 Physical 1 2 3 4 5 Energy 1 2 3 4 5 Mental 1 2 3 4 5 Head/Heart 1 2 3 4 5	**Sat 13 November** Emotion 1 2 3 4 5 Physical 1 2 3 4 5 Energy 1 2 3 4 5 Mental 1 2 3 4 5 Head/Heart 1 2 3 4 5	**Sun 21 November** Emotion 1 2 3 4 5 Physical 1 2 3 4 5 Energy 1 2 3 4 5 Mental 1 2 3 4 5 Head/Heart 1 2 3 4 5	**Mon 29 November** Emotion 1 2 3 4 5 Physical 1 2 3 4 5 Energy 1 2 3 4 5 Mental 1 2 3 4 5 Head/Heart 1 2 3 4 5
Mon 8 November Emotion 1 2 3 4 5 Physical 1 2 3 4 5 Energy 1 2 3 4 5 Mental 1 2 3 4 5 Head/Heart 1 2 3 4 5	**Sun 14 November** Emotion 1 2 3 4 5 Physical 1 2 3 4 5 Energy 1 2 3 4 5 Mental 1 2 3 4 5 Head/Heart 1 2 3 4 5	**Mon 22 November** Emotion 1 2 3 4 5 Physical 1 2 3 4 5 Energy 1 2 3 4 5 Mental 1 2 3 4 5 Head/Heart 1 2 3 4 5	**Tues 30 November** Emotion 1 2 3 4 5 Physical 1 2 3 4 5 Energy 1 2 3 4 5 Mental 1 2 3 4 5 Head/Heart 1 2 3 4 5
Tues 9 November Emotion 1 2 3 4 5 Physical 1 2 3 4 5 Energy 1 2 3 4 5 Mental 1 2 3 4 5 Head/Heart 1 2 3 4 5	**Mon 15 November** Emotion 1 2 3 4 5 Physical 1 2 3 4 5 Energy 1 2 3 4 5 Mental 1 2 3 4 5 Head/Heart 1 2 3 4 5	**Tues 23 November** Emotion 1 2 3 4 5 Physical 1 2 3 4 5 Energy 1 2 3 4 5 Mental 1 2 3 4 5 Head/Heart 1 2 3 4 5	**Wed 1 December** Emotion 1 2 3 4 5 Physical 1 2 3 4 5 Energy 1 2 3 4 5 Mental 1 2 3 4 5 Head/Heart 1 2 3 4 5
Wed 10 November Emotion 1 2 3 4 5 Physical 1 2 3 4 5 Energy 1 2 3 4 5 Mental 1 2 3 4 5 Head/Heart 1 2 3 4 5	**Tues 16 November** Emotion 1 2 3 4 5 Physical 1 2 3 4 5 Energy 1 2 3 4 5 Mental 1 2 3 4 5 Head/Heart 1 2 3 4 5	**Wed 24 November** Emotion 1 2 3 4 5 Physical 1 2 3 4 5 Energy 1 2 3 4 5 Mental 1 2 3 4 5 Head/Heart 1 2 3 4 5	**Thurs 2 December** Emotion 1 2 3 4 5 Physical 1 2 3 4 5 Energy 1 2 3 4 5 Mental 1 2 3 4 5 Head/Heart 1 2 3 4 5
	Wed 17 November Emotion 1 2 3 4 5 Physical 1 2 3 4 5 Energy 1 2 3 4 5 Mental 1 2 3 4 5 Head/Heart 1 2 3 4 5	**Thurs 25 November** Emotion 1 2 3 4 5 Physical 1 2 3 4 5 Energy 1 2 3 4 5 Mental 1 2 3 4 5 Head/Heart 1 2 3 4 5	**Fri 3 December** Emotion 1 2 3 4 5 Physical 1 2 3 4 5 Energy 1 2 3 4 5 Mental 1 2 3 4 5 Head/Heart 1 2 3 4 5
	Thurs 18 November Emotion 1 2 3 4 5 Physical 1 2 3 4 5 Energy 1 2 3 4 5 Mental 1 2 3 4 5 Head/Heart 1 2 3 4 5	**Fri 26 November** Emotion 1 2 3 4 5 Physical 1 2 3 4 5 Energy 1 2 3 4 5 Mental 1 2 3 4 5 Head/Heart 1 2 3 4 5	

Cycle 11

New Moon	First Quarter Moon	Full Moon	Last Quarter Moon
Sat 4 December Emotion 1 2 3 4 5 Physical 1 2 3 4 5 Energy 1 2 3 4 5 Mental 1 2 3 4 5 Head/Heart 1 2 3 4 5	**Sat 11 December** Emotion 1 2 3 4 5 Physical 1 2 3 4 5 Energy 1 2 3 4 5 Mental 1 2 3 4 5 Head/Heart 1 2 3 4 5	**Sun 19 December** Emotion 1 2 3 4 5 Physical 1 2 3 4 5 Energy 1 2 3 4 5 Mental 1 2 3 4 5 Head/Heart 1 2 3 4 5	**Mon 27 December** Emotion 1 2 3 4 5 Physical 1 2 3 4 5 Energy 1 2 3 4 5 Mental 1 2 3 4 5 Head/Heart 1 2 3 4 5
Sun 5 December Emotion 1 2 3 4 5 Physical 1 2 3 4 5 Energy 1 2 3 4 5 Mental 1 2 3 4 5 Head/Heart 1 2 3 4 5	**Sun 12 December** Emotion 1 2 3 4 5 Physical 1 2 3 4 5 Energy 1 2 3 4 5 Mental 1 2 3 4 5 Head/Heart 1 2 3 4 5	**Mon 20 December** Emotion 1 2 3 4 5 Physical 1 2 3 4 5 Energy 1 2 3 4 5 Mental 1 2 3 4 5 Head/Heart 1 2 3 4 5	**Tues 28 December** Emotion 1 2 3 4 5 Physical 1 2 3 4 5 Energy 1 2 3 4 5 Mental 1 2 3 4 5 Head/Heart 1 2 3 4 5
Mon 6 December Emotion 1 2 3 4 5 Physical 1 2 3 4 5 Energy 1 2 3 4 5 Mental 1 2 3 4 5 Head/Heart 1 2 3 4 5	**Mon 13 December** Emotion 1 2 3 4 5 Physical 1 2 3 4 5 Energy 1 2 3 4 5 Mental 1 2 3 4 5 Head/Heart 1 2 3 4 5	**Tues 21 December** Emotion 1 2 3 4 5 Physical 1 2 3 4 5 Energy 1 2 3 4 5 Mental 1 2 3 4 5 Head/Heart 1 2 3 4 5	**Wed 29 December** Emotion 1 2 3 4 5 Physical 1 2 3 4 5 Energy 1 2 3 4 5 Mental 1 2 3 4 5 Head/Heart 1 2 3 4 5
Tues 7 December Emotion 1 2 3 4 5 Physical 1 2 3 4 5 Energy 1 2 3 4 5 Mental 1 2 3 4 5 Head/Heart 1 2 3 4 5	**Tues 14 December** Emotion 1 2 3 4 5 Physical 1 2 3 4 5 Energy 1 2 3 4 5 Mental 1 2 3 4 5 Head/Heart 1 2 3 4 5	**Wed 22 December** Emotion 1 2 3 4 5 Physical 1 2 3 4 5 Energy 1 2 3 4 5 Mental 1 2 3 4 5 Head/Heart 1 2 3 4 5	**Thurs 30 December** Emotion 1 2 3 4 5 Physical 1 2 3 4 5 Energy 1 2 3 4 5 Mental 1 2 3 4 5 Head/Heart 1 2 3 4 5
Wed 8 December Emotion 1 2 3 4 5 Physical 1 2 3 4 5 Energy 1 2 3 4 5 Mental 1 2 3 4 5 Head/Heart 1 2 3 4 5	**Wed 15 December** Emotion 1 2 3 4 5 Physical 1 2 3 4 5 Energy 1 2 3 4 5 Mental 1 2 3 4 5 Head/Heart 1 2 3 4 5	**Thurs 23 December** Emotion 1 2 3 4 5 Physical 1 2 3 4 5 Energy 1 2 3 4 5 Mental 1 2 3 4 5 Head/Heart 1 2 3 4 5	**Fri 31 December** Emotion 1 2 3 4 5 Physical 1 2 3 4 5 Energy 1 2 3 4 5 Mental 1 2 3 4 5 Head/Heart 1 2 3 4 5
Thurs 9 December Emotion 1 2 3 4 5 Physical 1 2 3 4 5 Energy 1 2 3 4 5 Mental 1 2 3 4 5 Head/Heart 1 2 3 4 5	**Thurs 16 December** Emotion 1 2 3 4 5 Physical 1 2 3 4 5 Energy 1 2 3 4 5 Mental 1 2 3 4 5 Head/Heart 1 2 3 4 5	**Fri 24 December** Emotion 1 2 3 4 5 Physical 1 2 3 4 5 Energy 1 2 3 4 5 Mental 1 2 3 4 5 Head/Heart 1 2 3 4 5	**Sat 1 January** Emotion 1 2 3 4 5 Physical 1 2 3 4 5 Energy 1 2 3 4 5 Mental 1 2 3 4 5 Head/Heart 1 2 3 4 5
Fri 10 December Emotion 1 2 3 4 5 Physical 1 2 3 4 5 Energy 1 2 3 4 5 Mental 1 2 3 4 5 Head/Heart 1 2 3 4 5	**Fri 17 December** Emotion 1 2 3 4 5 Physical 1 2 3 4 5 Energy 1 2 3 4 5 Mental 1 2 3 4 5 Head/Heart 1 2 3 4 5	**Sat 25 December** Emotion 1 2 3 4 5 Physical 1 2 3 4 5 Energy 1 2 3 4 5 Mental 1 2 3 4 5 Head/Heart 1 2 3 4 5	**Sun 2 January** Emotion 1 2 3 4 5 Physical 1 2 3 4 5 Energy 1 2 3 4 5 Mental 1 2 3 4 5 Head/Heart 1 2 3 4 5
	Sat 18 December Emotion 1 2 3 4 5 Physical 1 2 3 4 5 Energy 1 2 3 4 5 Mental 1 2 3 4 5 Head/Heart 1 2 3 4 5	**Sun 26 December** Emotion 1 2 3 4 5 Physical 1 2 3 4 5 Energy 1 2 3 4 5 Mental 1 2 3 4 5 Head/Heart 1 2 3 4 5	

Cycle 12

New Moon	First Quarter Moon	Full Moon	Last Quarter Moon
Mon 3 January	**Mon 10 January**	**Tues 18 January**	**Wed 26 January**
Emotion 1 2 3 4 5	Emotion 1 2 3 4 5	Emotion 1 2 3 4 5	Emotion 1 2 3 4 5
Physical 1 2 3 4 5	Physical 1 2 3 4 5	Physical 1 2 3 4 5	Physical 1 2 3 4 5
Energy 1 2 3 4 5	Energy 1 2 3 4 5	Energy 1 2 3 4 5	Energy 1 2 3 4 5
Mental 1 2 3 4 5	Mental 1 2 3 4 5	Mental 1 2 3 4 5	Mental 1 2 3 4 5
Head/Heart 1 2 3 4 5	Head/Heart 1 2 3 4 5	Head/Heart 1 2 3 4 5	Head/Heart 1 2 3 4 5
Tues 4 January	**Tues 11 January**	**Wed 19 January**	**Thurs 27 January**
Emotion 1 2 3 4 5	Emotion 1 2 3 4 5	Emotion 1 2 3 4 5	Emotion 1 2 3 4 5
Physical 1 2 3 4 5	Physical 1 2 3 4 5	Physical 1 2 3 4 5	Physical 1 2 3 4 5
Energy 1 2 3 4 5	Energy 1 2 3 4 5	Energy 1 2 3 4 5	Energy 1 2 3 4 5
Mental 1 2 3 4 5	Mental 1 2 3 4 5	Mental 1 2 3 4 5	Mental 1 2 3 4 5
Head/Heart 1 2 3 4 5	Head/Heart 1 2 3 4 5	Head/Heart 1 2 3 4 5	Head/Heart 1 2 3 4 5
Wed 5 January	**Wed 12 January**	**Thurs 20 January**	**Fri 28 January**
Emotion 1 2 3 4 5	Emotion 1 2 3 4 5	Emotion 1 2 3 4 5	Emotion 1 2 3 4 5
Physical 1 2 3 4 5	Physical 1 2 3 4 5	Physical 1 2 3 4 5	Physical 1 2 3 4 5
Energy 1 2 3 4 5	Energy 1 2 3 4 5	Energy 1 2 3 4 5	Energy 1 2 3 4 5
Mental 1 2 3 4 5	Mental 1 2 3 4 5	Mental 1 2 3 4 5	Mental 1 2 3 4 5
Head/Heart 1 2 3 4 5	Head/Heart 1 2 3 4 5	Head/Heart 1 2 3 4 5	Head/Heart 1 2 3 4 5
Thurs 6 January	**Thurs 13 January**	**Fri 21 January**	**Sat 29 January**
Emotion 1 2 3 4 5	Emotion 1 2 3 4 5	Emotion 1 2 3 4 5	Emotion 1 2 3 4 5
Physical 1 2 3 4 5	Physical 1 2 3 4 5	Physical 1 2 3 4 5	Physical 1 2 3 4 5
Energy 1 2 3 4 5	Energy 1 2 3 4 5	Energy 1 2 3 4 5	Energy 1 2 3 4 5
Mental 1 2 3 4 5	Mental 1 2 3 4 5	Mental 1 2 3 4 5	Mental 1 2 3 4 5
Head/Heart 1 2 3 4 5	Head/Heart 1 2 3 4 5	Head/Heart 1 2 3 4 5	Head/Heart 1 2 3 4 5
Fri 7 January	**Fri 14 January**	**Sat 22 January**	**Sun 30 January**
Emotion 1 2 3 4 5	Emotion 1 2 3 4 5	Emotion 1 2 3 4 5	Emotion 1 2 3 4 5
Physical 1 2 3 4 5	Physical 1 2 3 4 5	Physical 1 2 3 4 5	Physical 1 2 3 4 5
Energy 1 2 3 4 5	Energy 1 2 3 4 5	Energy 1 2 3 4 5	Energy 1 2 3 4 5
Mental 1 2 3 4 5	Mental 1 2 3 4 5	Mental 1 2 3 4 5	Mental 1 2 3 4 5
Head/Heart 1 2 3 4 5	Head/Heart 1 2 3 4 5	Head/Heart 1 2 3 4 5	Head/Heart 1 2 3 4 5
Sat 8 January	**Sat 15 January**	**Sun 23 January**	**Mon 31 January**
Emotion 1 2 3 4 5	Emotion 1 2 3 4 5	Emotion 1 2 3 4 5	Emotion 1 2 3 4 5
Physical 1 2 3 4 5	Physical 1 2 3 4 5	Physical 1 2 3 4 5	Physical 1 2 3 4 5
Energy 1 2 3 4 5	Energy 1 2 3 4 5	Energy 1 2 3 4 5	Energy 1 2 3 4 5
Mental 1 2 3 4 5	Mental 1 2 3 4 5	Mental 1 2 3 4 5	Mental 1 2 3 4 5
Head/Heart 1 2 3 4 5	Head/Heart 1 2 3 4 5	Head/Heart 1 2 3 4 5	Head/Heart 1 2 3 4 5
Sun 9 January	**Sun 16 January**	**Mon 24 January**	
Emotion 1 2 3 4 5	Emotion 1 2 3 4 5	Emotion 1 2 3 4 5	
Physical 1 2 3 4 5	Physical 1 2 3 4 5	Physical 1 2 3 4 5	
Energy 1 2 3 4 5	Energy 1 2 3 4 5	Energy 1 2 3 4 5	
Mental 1 2 3 4 5	Mental 1 2 3 4 5	Mental 1 2 3 4 5	
Head/Heart 1 2 3 4 5	Head/Heart 1 2 3 4 5	Head/Heart 1 2 3 4 5	
	Mon 17 January	**Tues 25 January**	
	Emotion 1 2 3 4 5	Emotion 1 2 3 4 5	
	Physical 1 2 3 4 5	Physical 1 2 3 4 5	
	Energy 1 2 3 4 5	Energy 1 2 3 4 5	
	Mental 1 2 3 4 5	Mental 1 2 3 4 5	
	Head/Heart 1 2 3 4 5	Head/Heart 1 2 3 4 5	

Cycle 13

New Moon	First Quarter Moon	Full Moon	Last Quarter Moon
Tues 1 February	Wed 9 February	Thurs 17 February	Thurs 24 February
Emotion 1 2 3 4 5 Physical 1 2 3 4 5 Energy 1 2 3 4 5 Mental 1 2 3 4 5 Head/Heart 1 2 3 4 5	Emotion 1 2 3 4 5 Physical 1 2 3 4 5 Energy 1 2 3 4 5 Mental 1 2 3 4 5 Head/Heart 1 2 3 4 5	Emotion 1 2 3 4 5 Physical 1 2 3 4 5 Energy 1 2 3 4 5 Mental 1 2 3 4 5 Head/Heart 1 2 3 4 5	Emotion 1 2 3 4 5 Physical 1 2 3 4 5 Energy 1 2 3 4 5 Mental 1 2 3 4 5 Head/Heart 1 2 3 4 5
Wed 2 February	Thurs 10 February	Fri 18 February	Fri 25 February
Emotion 1 2 3 4 5 Physical 1 2 3 4 5 Energy 1 2 3 4 5 Mental 1 2 3 4 5 Head/Heart 1 2 3 4 5	Emotion 1 2 3 4 5 Physical 1 2 3 4 5 Energy 1 2 3 4 5 Mental 1 2 3 4 5 Head/Heart 1 2 3 4 5	Emotion 1 2 3 4 5 Physical 1 2 3 4 5 Energy 1 2 3 4 5 Mental 1 2 3 4 5 Head/Heart 1 2 3 4 5	Emotion 1 2 3 4 5 Physical 1 2 3 4 5 Energy 1 2 3 4 5 Mental 1 2 3 4 5 Head/Heart 1 2 3 4 5
Thurs 3 February	Fri 11 February	Sat 19 February	Sat 26 February
Emotion 1 2 3 4 5 Physical 1 2 3 4 5 Energy 1 2 3 4 5 Mental 1 2 3 4 5 Head/Heart 1 2 3 4 5	Emotion 1 2 3 4 5 Physical 1 2 3 4 5 Energy 1 2 3 4 5 Mental 1 2 3 4 5 Head/Heart 1 2 3 4 5	Emotion 1 2 3 4 5 Physical 1 2 3 4 5 Energy 1 2 3 4 5 Mental 1 2 3 4 5 Head/Heart 1 2 3 4 5	Emotion 1 2 3 4 5 Physical 1 2 3 4 5 Energy 1 2 3 4 5 Mental 1 2 3 4 5 Head/Heart 1 2 3 4 5
Fri 4 February	Sat 12 February	Sun 20 February	Sun 27 February
Emotion 1 2 3 4 5 Physical 1 2 3 4 5 Energy 1 2 3 4 5 Mental 1 2 3 4 5 Head/Heart 1 2 3 4 5	Emotion 1 2 3 4 5 Physical 1 2 3 4 5 Energy 1 2 3 4 5 Mental 1 2 3 4 5 Head/Heart 1 2 3 4 5	Emotion 1 2 3 4 5 Physical 1 2 3 4 5 Energy 1 2 3 4 5 Mental 1 2 3 4 5 Head/Heart 1 2 3 4 5	Emotion 1 2 3 4 5 Physical 1 2 3 4 5 Energy 1 2 3 4 5 Mental 1 2 3 4 5 Head/Heart 1 2 3 4 5
Sat 5 February	Sun 13 February	Mon 21 February	Mon 28 February
Emotion 1 2 3 4 5 Physical 1 2 3 4 5 Energy 1 2 3 4 5 Mental 1 2 3 4 5 Head/Heart 1 2 3 4 5	Emotion 1 2 3 4 5 Physical 1 2 3 4 5 Energy 1 2 3 4 5 Mental 1 2 3 4 5 Head/Heart 1 2 3 4 5	Emotion 1 2 3 4 5 Physical 1 2 3 4 5 Energy 1 2 3 4 5 Mental 1 2 3 4 5 Head/Heart 1 2 3 4 5	Emotion 1 2 3 4 5 Physical 1 2 3 4 5 Energy 1 2 3 4 5 Mental 1 2 3 4 5 Head/Heart 1 2 3 4 5
Sun 6 February	Mon 14 February	Tues 22 February	Tues 1 March
Emotion 1 2 3 4 5 Physical 1 2 3 4 5 Energy 1 2 3 4 5 Mental 1 2 3 4 5 Head/Heart 1 2 3 4 5	Emotion 1 2 3 4 5 Physical 1 2 3 4 5 Energy 1 2 3 4 5 Mental 1 2 3 4 5 Head/Heart 1 2 3 4 5	Emotion 1 2 3 4 5 Physical 1 2 3 4 5 Energy 1 2 3 4 5 Mental 1 2 3 4 5 Head/Heart 1 2 3 4 5	Emotion 1 2 3 4 5 Physical 1 2 3 4 5 Energy 1 2 3 4 5 Mental 1 2 3 4 5 Head/Heart 1 2 3 4 5
Mon 7 February	Tues 15 February	Wed 23 February	Wed 2 March
Emotion 1 2 3 4 5 Physical 1 2 3 4 5 Energy 1 2 3 4 5 Mental 1 2 3 4 5 Head/Heart 1 2 3 4 5	Emotion 1 2 3 4 5 Physical 1 2 3 4 5 Energy 1 2 3 4 5 Mental 1 2 3 4 5 Head/Heart 1 2 3 4 5	Emotion 1 2 3 4 5 Physical 1 2 3 4 5 Energy 1 2 3 4 5 Mental 1 2 3 4 5 Head/Heart 1 2 3 4 5	Emotion 1 2 3 4 5 Physical 1 2 3 4 5 Energy 1 2 3 4 5 Mental 1 2 3 4 5 Head/Heart 1 2 3 4 5
Tues 8 February	Wed 16 February		
Emotion 1 2 3 4 5 Physical 1 2 3 4 5 Energy 1 2 3 4 5 Mental 1 2 3 4 5 Head/Heart 1 2 3 4 5	Emotion 1 2 3 4 5 Physical 1 2 3 4 5 Energy 1 2 3 4 5 Mental 1 2 3 4 5 Head/Heart 1 2 3 4 5		

2021 Lunar New Year Intentions

Intentions

Friday 12 February

My Lunar New Year

Just as New Year's Eve in the solar calendar is a time of reflection and intention setting for the year ahead, so too is the Lunar New Year.

However, unlike a new year's resolution that rarely sees more than a weeks' worth of commitment, by taking the time to reflect on our intentions, desires, and values we start to uncover the goals and dreams for the year ahead that are deeply embedded within our heart and soul. As these intentions come from the heart rather than the head they are harder to put aside, and either consciously or unconsciously, we will endeavour to meet those goals as best we can throughout the year.

Over the years I have written intentions for the year in this way many times, often without referring back to them until years end. However, in reviewing them I have found many times that I have lived up to the intentions and goals I had set for myself each time.

The following pages contain twenty-four questions across twelve areas of life to encourage you to reflect on how you would like your 2021 Lunar Year to manifest. These questions are designed to help you to bring light into places you may not have previously given much thought to, as well as to shine a different perspective on areas of well-worn travel.

The areas that will be covered are:

1. Physical Health
2. Mental and Cognitive Health
3. Abundance and Lifestyle
4. Safety and Security
5. Environment
6. Play
7. Communication
8. Relationships
9. Self-Responsibility and Love
10. Community
11. Authenticity, and
12. Finding Meaning

You may like to set aside some time when you can complete these questions in a quiet and safe space, either in one sitting or spread out over a few sessions.

I encourage you to complete all the questions, your answers don't have to be long or detailed, a sentence or two will do. The power is in the reflection, the time to consider each question for yourself and for the year ahead. Your journal will then act as a prompt to bring you back to your intentions throughout the year.

Take as much time as you need with each question and don't be afraid to answer it honestly, even if the answer scares you or makes you uncomfortable. This is your private space where you can be completely open and honest with yourself about your dreams and intentions.

The following pages provide information about each question, use this to provide prompts for writing down your answers on pages 61 to 72.

Physical Health

1. My Health and Wellbeing

How might I be a healthier me? What changes can you make in your life that will help you to be a physically healthier you. Do you want to do more exercise, change your eating or drinking habits? Do you want to follow up on medical or alternate health professional appointments? Do you want more sleep or more rest?

Sometimes it is hard to make big changes to support our health and wellbeing, but changes don't have to be big or dramatic. You can focus your attention on what is achievable; either a small change (eg walk the dog one day per week) or change in just one area of your life (eg improve my eating habits). Small incremental changes can lead to much longer lasting change over time.

Mental and Cognitive Health

2. My Mental Health

What do I need to support my mental health? Mental health refers to our state of mind and how it effects our day to day life. Mental illness can manifest as a diagnosed medical condition such as depression or bi polar etc, or as the experience of high levels of anxiety, stress or other mental anguish. Mental health is vital to our overall health and wellbeing however, can often be ignored or down played by ourself or others around us.

Are you doing everything you need to, to stay mentally well, however this looks for you? Whether your chosen mental health treatment is through medication and/or other avenues of mainstream or alternate healing, are you placing your mental health as a priority and doing everything you need to do?

3. My Cognitive Health

Cognitive health is our mental ability and agility, our capacity to think, remember and process information. What do you need to do to maintain or develop your cognitive health? Do you need to stretch a little and learn something new? Develop a new hobby or start a new course of learning? Would you benefit from some regular crosswords or other brain stretching exercise? Or do you need to rest your mind, allow it to stop thinking and doing, to trust you are safe enough to let go and be still and quiet for a time?

Abundance and Lifestyle

4. My Lifestyle

Am living my most authentic and impeccable life? Does your lifestyle reflect the life you want to be living, the person you know yourself to be? What changes can you make in your life this year to bring yourself into greater alignment with your most authentic life.

5. My Belongings

How will I view my belongings in 2021? In our highly materialistic world, it is worth taking time to examine what priority we place on our belongings, and on what we own that is truly important to us. Reflect on what attitude towards belongings you are taking into 2021. Do you have enough material items? Do you honour, care for, and respect the things that you own? Do you reuse, repair and recycle? What value do you place or new v's old? Are there possessions you would like to get rid of or give away or sell? How well do you care for the things that you cherish? Reflect on your values in relation to belongings, and ask yourself if your lived life is consistent with these values.

6. My Finance and Career

What are my intentions for my finance and career? We all need money in our current society to survive, and we all deserve a share of the economy we live in. Don't be afraid to set financial targets or to dream big for your future. The possession of money is not the root of all evil. It is what we do with it that counts, not how much of it we have. Think about the practical steps needed to reach your financial goals, make them part of your focus for the year ahead. What could you create in the world if you had enough money do with what you would like?

7. My Education

What do I want to learn this year? Learning is a lifelong journey and can take place in many settings not just academic ones. There are also many ways to learn. We can learn through doing, listening, watching, and reading. Take time to reflect on how you can expand your experience and understanding of life through learning this year.

Safety and Security

8. My Trust

In what or whom do I place my trust? Trust is an important part of day to day life, even though it may not be something we spend much time thinking about. We trust each night we will wake up in the morning, we trust we will be kept safe as we travel to and from home, we trust our family and friends will continue to care for us, we trust our bodies will not get sick or fail us, we trust we will be held safe through the storm. Or, maybe you don't feel much trust for some or any of these things? Who and what do you trust? Who and what do you rely on? Take time to acknowledge who and what you place your trust in, and who and what helps you to feel safe.

Environment

9. My Sustainable Life

How might I live a more sustainable life in 2021? Am I connected with nature in the ways I wish to be? Mother nature is calling for us to nurture her, and through her, nurture ourselves. How might you choose to live more sustainably each day? What might you be able to do to love, appreciate and connect with nature in the ways that you wish to?

Play

10. My Creative Expression

What is my creative expression? Being able to express our creativity is important for our mental, emotional and soulful wellbeing. Creativity can show itself in traditional artistic expression, but also in other pursuits such as; gardening, building, cooking, designing parties and events, play and much more. Anything that requires us to think outside of our day to day routine, anything that allows our mind, heart and soul to roam free and explore, allows us to express our creativity. What expressions of creativity call to you in 2021?

Authenticity

11. My Hearts Calling

What is my heart longing for in 2021? What am I being called to; do, be, feel, share, create, learn, heal? The hearts calling is that still small voice that sings to us in the quiet, it is where flow and ease resides. It is what tugs at our soul to be fulfilled and is not connected to 'should' or feelings of duty, but born of longing and deep knowing. Listen to your heart, what is it asking of you?

12. My Boundaries

What values define me? We all have values we live by, but for most of us they are never explored, made conscious and named. To understand our values helps us to understand our boundaries, in relationship to our self and to others. Often when our boundaries are crossed, we fail to recognise that it has even occurred, experiencing it only as a feeling of unease, which is then dismissed as unimportant or too difficult to articulate. However, when we give name to our values it is easier to put language to our boundaries so that they may be heard, felt and honoured.

Brene Brown in her book Dare to Lead says that we all have one or two core values that underpin how we move through life, when we identify what these values are it helps us to honour who we are and what we expect from our self and others.

When we have identified our values, we are able to hold both ourselves and others accountable to the deeply held boundaries required by these values. For 2021 you may wish to focus on one of your core values and how you plan to honour it more fully. Or you may choose to pick another value that you would like to enhance or learn to lean into throughout the year. Become aware throughout the year how that value is upheld or ignored by those around you and how it relates to your feeling of boundaries.

Communication

13. My Truth

What do I believe to be true? What gives my life meaning? Our truth speaks to what we value and what we believe about life. Is life friendly? Is love important? Do I value family, friendships? Is my work or career important? Do I believe financial security is important to my happiness? Our truth can and does change depending on our life circumstances, age, health, mental and emotional wellbeing, and our spiritual beliefs. Ask yourself what is true for you right now, and what you want to be true to in 2021.

Relationships

14. My Kindness

How will I be kind? Kindness can be felt as an both outward and inward expression of Love. When our kindness comes from an open and willing heart, we offer an outward expression of Loving presence. When we are kind to ourselves, we embrace the opportunity for inward loving self-care. How either of these expressions looks and feels will depend on both your own and others needs at the time. Kindness can be a movement towards someone, an act of generosity or service, a gift, a smile a hug, or an act of self-care. Or it may be a movement away, from a person, a job or a circumstance. Kindness can be both an absence or presence, and as long as they come from Love both are equally of worth. Ask yourself how you would like kindness to show up in 2021, both for yourself and for those around you.

15. My Loving Connections

Which relationships in my life need care and attention this year? Consider not just your relationships with others, but also with yourself. When we live in loving relationship with our self we have a greater capacity to pour that love out to those around us. Are there new relationships that you would like to call into your life; an intimate partner, a business relationship, new friendships? Set your intention to call in those new relationships or take time in valuing existing ones.

16. My Intimacy

What are my expectations and desires in relation to intimacy? What are my intimacy patterns of behaviour? Do these behaviours work for me and for my partner or future partner? What does your ideal intimate relationship look and feel like? We all have patterns and behaviours that repeat from one intimate relationship to the next, this is why we often attract the same type of person and find ourselves in the same type of intimate relationship over and over again. To break the cycle, we need to change these patterns and behaviours. Even in a stable long-term relationship we can find ourselves repeating the same cycle of behaviours over and over again. What, if anything, is in need of change in your life in terms of your intimate relationships? Remember you are only responsible for, and have control over, you and how you choose to show up. So, where can you make change to your behaviours, attitude, energy and thoughts in terms of your intimate relationships?

Self-Responsibility and Growth

17. My Healing

How will I show up for my healing in 2021? Healing is a lifelong journey. We all carry the wounds and scars of childhood, of past relationships, grief and loss, and our healing requires a deep inward journey into our own pain and messiness. It takes courage, consistency and commitment to journey the spiral of healing as it regularly brings us back to revisit old wounds again and again for deeper and deeper healing. What are your intentions for deeper healing this year? How will you support yourself as you dive deeper into this process? Who do you need to help you navigate the darkness and support your path back to the light?

18. My Personal Growth

Where are my areas for personal growth? What areas of your life are seeking growth and new learning? Where are the areas you can or need to stretch your wings in order to expand your horizons? What is in need of being seen to be your most authentic and impeccable you? Where can you break old patterns, make different choices, learn more about yourself and how you move through the world?

19. My Gratitude

What am I grateful for in 2021? How will I express or show my gratitude? Gratitude is a powerful tool for healing, it not only helps lead us into greater appreciation for all the positive things that we have in our life, but also for the teaching and growth that comes from the messy, hard and painful experiences. When we start each day with a grateful heart it is easier to see more and things to be grateful for as we move through our day. Gratitude also helps us to see those people and circumstances that are supporting us through the hard times. How will you bring gratitude into your life this coming year?

Community

20. My Generosity or Service

How will my generosity express itself this year? How might I serve the world around me? "The best way to find yourself is to lose yourself in the service of others." *Mahatma Gandhi*. Giving of ourselves; our time, our money, our skills, our presence, serves both the giver and the receiver. Through service we grow, it teaches us more about what it is to receive, and through giving, the value of what we each have within us to offer the world. Your service in 2021 may be generosity to others or to yourself or to both.

21. My Community

Who is in your community? These are people in life that make up your circle of friends and family on which you depend. These are the people you trust and can turn to for support and help. These are also the people who depend on you for care and support. One way to approach this section is to draw a mind map, with yourself at the centre and the names of the members of your community around you, those who you trust the most place closer to you, those less so further away, note any feelings or memories that arise as you do this exercise. Are there people you would like to be closer in your map, or further away? How might you go about making that happen?

22. My Giveaway

What is my giveaway this year? Your giveaway can be an attitude, a feeling, a thing, an idea, a belief, anything that no longer serves your most authentic life. What will your giveaway be?

Finding Meaning

23. My Soul

What does my soul yearn for? In what ways does my soul need nourishing? Our soulful or spiritual journey is as important to our overall wellbeing as our mental, physical and emotional health. Lean into what your soul desires in order to be fed.

24. My Faith

This section is a place for text or imagery relating to your beliefs or understandings of how and why the world is the way it is. You can use it according to what fits with your soul or faith expression. It is an opportunity to create a vision of your future for 2021 for you to come back to during times of darkness or when you need inspiration throughout the year ahead.

2021 Lunar New Year Intentions

Physical Health

1. My Health and Wellbeing
How might I be a healthier me?

Mental and Cognitive Health

2. My Mental Health
What do I need to support my mental health?

3. My Cognitive Health
What do I need to do to maintain or develop my cognitive health?

Abundance and Lifestyle

4. My Lifestyle
How might I live my most authentic and impeccable life?

5. My Belongings
How will I view my belongings in 2021?

6. My Finance and Career
What are my intentions for my finance and career?

7. My Education
What do I want to learn this year?

Safety and Security
8. My Trust
In what or whom do I place my trust?

Environment

9. My Sustainable Life

How might will I live a more sustainable life in 2021?

Play

10. My Creative Expression

What is my creative expression?

Authenticity

11. My Hearts Calling

What is my heart longing for in 2021?

12. My Boundaries

What values define me?

Communication

13. My Truth

What do I believe to be true?

Relationships

14. My Kindness

How will I be kind?

15. My Loving Connections
Which relationships in my life need care and attention this year?

16. My Intimacy
What are my expectations and desires in relation to intimacy?

Self-Responsibility and Growth

17. My Healing

How will I show up for my healing in 2021?

18. My Personal Growth

Where are my areas for personal growth?

19. My Gratitude

What am I grateful for in 2021?

Community

20. My Generosity or Service

How will my generosity express itself this year?

21. My Community

Who is in my community?

Putting yourself in the middle create a mind map of people in your community (including family). The ones closest to you in in trust, love, respect, and caring being the ones placed closest to you in the diagram. Draw lines around specific groups or between connections. Make it as creative or colourful as you like. Become aware of where you place people, and how comfortable or uncomfortable that feels for you. Listen to what you heart and body is telling you as you create this map.

Me

22. My Giveaway

What is my giveaway this year?

Finding Meaning

23. My Soul

What does my soul yearn for?

24. My Faith

Some ways of creating your faith vision for 2021 include:

- using oracle or tarot cards (Lunar Cycle and 13 Cycle reading spreads are provided in the following pages)
- write out a piece of text from a book of faith or learning,
- write out a quote or poem or inspirational piece that resonates for you, or
- do a vision board and paste a copy in this space of your Journal

Whatever way you choose, make is personal to you and a true reflection of your faith whether that be esoteric, or science based or a combination of both or neither.

My Faith 2021:

Lunar Cycle Reading

1. **The New Moon** ~ Hearts Calling
   This is the lesson, the truth of your hearts calling, it is your foundation to keep coming back to throughout this lunar year.

2. **The Waxing Moon** ~ Past
   What you are hanging onto, the pieces of your past that are influencing how or whether you can move towards your hearts calling

3. **The First Quarter Moon** ~ Present
   What is occurring in your life right now.

4. **The Full Moon** ~ Blessings
   What gifts and blessings that are being offered to support you in this journey.

5. **The Last Quarter Moon** ~ Releasing
   What needs to be released in order for you to move forward.

6. **The Waning Moon** ~ Fulfillment
   The outcome of this journey, the culmination of the lesson of your hearts calling.

1. The New Moon ~ Hearts Calling

2. The Waxing Moon ~ Past

3. The First Quarter Moon ~ Present

4. The Full Moon ~ Blessings

5. The Last Quarter Moon ~ Releasing

6. The Waning Moon ~ Fulfillment

13 Cycle Oracle Reading
Simply choose one card for each cycle of the Lunar Year.

1st Cycle

2nd Cycle

3rd Cycle

4th Cycle

5th Cycle

6th Cycle

7th Cycle

8th Cycle

9th Cycle

10th Cycle

11th Cycle

12th Cycle

13th Cycle

Lunar Cycle 1

Friday 12 February to Friday 12 March 2021

New Moon Manifesting

New Beginnings – Lunar New Year

Friday 12 February 2021 – Southern
Thursday 11 February 2021 – Northern

What are your intentions for the coming lunar cycle?

- Physical Health
- Mental and Cognitive Health
- Abundance and Lifestyle
- Safety and Security
- Environment
- Play
- Authenticity
- Communication
- Relationships
- Self-Responsibility and Growth
- Community
- Finding Meaning

My Faith:

Use this section for a card reading, bible verse or quote that speaks to you.

My Journaling

Friday 12 February to Friday 19 February 2021 - Southern
Thursday 11 February to Friday 18 February 2021 – Northern

Mercury in Retrograde: Full 31 January to 21 February in Aquarius

New Moon
Fri 12 Feb
Thurs 11 Feb

Journaling prompt: Write the words you most need to hear.

First Quarter Moon Power Up

Moving Forward
Saturday 20 February 2021 – Southern
Friday 19 February 2021 – Northern

What actions will you take now to move your intentions forward?

- Physical Health
- Mental and Cognitive Health
- Abundance and Lifestyle
- Safety and Security
- Environment
- Play
- Authenticity
- Communication
- Relationships
- Self-Responsibility and Growth
- Community
- Finding Meaning

My Journaling

Saturday 20 February to Friday 26 February 2021 - Southern
Friday 19 February to Friday 26 February 2021 – Northern

Mercury in Retrograde: Post: 22 February to 12 March in Aquarius

First Quarter Moon
Sat 20 Feb
Fri 19 Feb

Journaling prompt: What is the best advice you have ever been given?

Full Moon Celebration

The Harvest
Saturday 27 February 2021 – Southern
Saturday 27 February 2021 – Northern

What am I celebrating and reaping the harvest of this Full Moon?

- Physical Health
- Mental and Cognitive Health
- Abundance and Lifestyle
- Safety and Security
- Environment
- Play
- Authenticity
- Communication
- Relationships
- Self-Responsibility and Growth
- Community
- Finding Meaning

The full moon in February

The Red Moon in the **Southern Hemisphere;** rises in February, often appearing reddish through a scorching haze of summer heat.

The Snow Moon in the **Northern Hemisphere;** appears when the snow is deepest, thus this is a time for home, hearth, and family.

My Journaling

Saturday 27 February to Friday 5 March 2021 - Southern
Saturday 27 February to Friday 5 March 2021 - Northern

Mercury in Retrograde: Post: 22 February to 12 March in Aquarius

Full Moon
Sat 27 Feb

Journaling prompt: How do you see yourself? How do you think others see you?

Third Quarter Moon Releasing

Letting It Go
Saturday 6 March 2021 – Southern
Saturday 6 March 2021 – Northern

At this time of the Third Quarter Moon I see, acknowledge and release...

- Physical Health
- Mental and Cognitive Health
- Abundance and Lifestyle
- Safety and Security
- Environment
- Play
- Authenticity
- Communication
- Relationships
- Self-Responsibility and Growth
- Community
- Finding Meaning

My Journaling

Saturday 6 March to Friday 12 March 2021 - Southern
Saturday 6 March to Friday 12 March 2021 - Northern

Mercury in Retrograde: Post: 22 February to 12 March in Aquarius

Third Quarter
Moon
Sat 6 Mar

Journaling prompt: What does love mean to me?

Lunar Cycle 2

Saturday 13 March to Sunday 11 April 2021

New Moon Manifesting

New Beginnings
Saturday 13 March 2021 – Southern
Saturday 13 March 2021 – Northern

What are your intentions for the coming lunar cycle?

- Physical Health
- Mental and Cognitive Health
- Abundance and Lifestyle
- Safety and Security
- Environment
- Play
- Authenticity
- Communication
- Relationships
- Self-Responsibility and Growth
- Community
- Finding Meaning

My Faith:

Use this section for a card reading, bible verse or quote that speaks to you.

My Journaling

Saturday 13 March to Sunday 21 March 2021 - Southern
Saturday 13 March to Sunday 21 March 2021 - Northern

New Moon
Sat 13 March

Journaling prompt: What beliefs or fears are causing resistance?

First Quarter Moon Power Up

Moving Forward

Monday 22 March 2021 – Southern
Monday 21 March 2021 – Northern

What actions will you take now to move your intentions forward?

- Physical Health
- Mental and Cognitive Health
- Abundance and Lifestyle
- Safety and Security
- Environment
- Play
- Authenticity
- Communication
- Relationships
- Self-Responsibility and Growth
- Community
- Finding Meaning

My Journaling

Monday 22 March to Sunday 28 March 2021 - Southern
Sunday 21 March to Sunday 28 March 2021 – Northern

First Quarter Moon
Mon 22 March
Sun 21 March

Journaling prompt: How can I forgive myself today? I forgive myself for...

Full Moon Celebration

The Harvest

Monday 29 March 2021 – Southern
Monday 29 March 2021 – Northern

What am I celebrating and reaping the harvest of this Full Moon?

- Physical Health
- Mental and Cognitive Health
- Abundance and Lifestyle
- Safety and Security
- Environment
- Play
- Authenticity
- Communication
- Relationships
- Self-Responsibility and Growth
- Community
- Finding Meaning

The full moon in March

The Full Fruit Moon in the **Southern Hemisphere**; is appropriately named after the wide variety of fruits harvested during March.

The Sap Moon in the **Northern Hemisphere**; as the trees warm and the sap rises, the ground also softens and worms begin to burrow out of the ground, thus this time may also be named the Worm Moon.

My Journaling

Monday 29 March to Saturday 3 April 2021 - Southern
Monday 29 March to Saturday 3 April 2021 - Northern

Full Moon
Mon 29 March

Journaling prompt: Knowing I create my reality... today I create...
(from Emma Queen's Living with intention - 7 day journaling program)

Third Quarter Moon Releasing

Letting It Go

Sunday 4 April 2021 – Southern – *Autumn Equinox*
Sunday 4 April 2021 – Northern – *Spring Equinox*

At this time of the Third Quarter Moon I see, acknowledge and release...

- Physical Health
- Mental and Cognitive Health
- Abundance and Lifestyle
- Safety and Security
- Environment
- Play
- Authenticity
- Communication
- Relationships
- Self-Responsibility and Growth
- Community
- Finding Meaning

My Journaling

Sunday 4 April to Sunday 11 April 2021 - Southern
Sunday 4 April to Sunday 11 April 2021 - Northern

Third Quarter
Moon
Sun 4 April

Journaling prompt: If I could talk to my teenage self, the one thing I would say is...

Lunar Cycle 3

Monday 12 April to Tuesday 11 May 2021

New Moon Manifesting

New Beginnings
Monday 12 April 2021 – Southern
Monday 12 April 2021 – Northern

What are your intentions for the coming lunar cycle?

- Physical Health
- Mental and Cognitive Health
- Abundance and Lifestyle
- Safety and Security
- Environment
- Play
- Authenticity
- Communication
- Relationships
- Self-Responsibility and Growth
- Community
- Finding Meaning

My Faith:

Use this section for a card reading, bible verse or quote that speaks to you.

My Journaling

Monday 12 April to Monday 19 April 2021 - Southern
Monday 12 April to Monday 19 April 2021 - Northern

New Moon
Mon 12 April

Journaling prompt: What does authentic love look like for me?

First Quarter Moon Power Up

Moving Forward
Tuesday 20 April 2021 – Southern
Tues 20 April 2021 – Northern

What actions will you take now to move your intentions forward?

- Physical Health
- Mental and Cognitive Health
- Abundance and Lifestyle
- Safety and Security
- Environment
- Play
- Authenticity
- Communication
- Relationships
- Self-Responsibility and Growth
- Community
- Finding Meaning

My Journaling

Tuesday 20 April to Monday 26 April 2021 - Southern
Tuesday 20 April to Monday 26 April 2021 – Northern

20 to 23 April
Autumn Equinox – Alban Elfed, - Southern
Spring Equinox - Alban Eilir - Northern

First Quarter Moon
Mon 26 April

Journaling prompt: What do you love about life?

Full Moon Celebration

The Harvest
Tuesday 27 April 2021 **Super Moon** – Southern
Tuesday 27 April 2021 **Super Moon** – Northern

What am I celebrating and reaping the harvest of this Full Moon?

- Physical Health
- Mental and Cognitive Health
- Abundance and Lifestyle
- Safety and Security
- Environments
- Play
- Authenticity
- Communication
- Relationships
- Self-Responsibility and Growth
- Community
- Finding Meaning

The full moon in April

The Harvest Moon in the **Southern Hemisphere;** is when the harvest of crops usually gets into full swing.

The Pink Moon in the **Northern Hemisphere;** is the time many flowers turn pink and bloom.

My Journaling

Tuesday 27 April to Monday 3 May 2021 - Southern
Tuesday 27 April to Monday 3 May 2021 - Northern

1 May
Samhain (Halloween), the beginning of Winter - Southern
Beltane, the beginning of Summer - Northern

Full Moon
Tues 267 April

Journaling prompt: Write a list of questions to which you urgently need answers

Third Quarter Moon Releasing

Letting It Go

Tuesday 4 May 2021 – Southern

Monday 3 May 2021 – Northern

At this time of the Third Quarter Moon I see, acknowledge and release...

- Physical Health
- Mental and Cognitive Health
- Abundance and Lifestyle
- Safety and Security
- Environment
- Play
- Authenticity
- Communication
- Relationships
- Self-Responsibility and Growth
- Community
- Finding Meaning

My Journaling

Tuesday 4 May to Tuesday 11 May 2021 - Southern
Monday 3 May to Tuesday 11 May 2021 - Northern

Third Quarter
Moon
Tues 4 May
Mon 3 May

Journaling prompt: Dear Past Me ... Dear Future Me.

Lunar Cycle 4

Wednesday 12 May to Wednesday 9 June 2021

New Moon Manifesting

New Beginnings
Wednesday 12 May 2021 – Southern
Tuesday 11 May 2021 – Northern

What are your intentions for the coming lunar cycle?

- Physical Health
- Mental and Cognitive Health
- Abundance and Lifestyle
- Safety and Security
- Environment
- Play
- Authenticity
- Communication
- Relationships
- Self-Responsibility and Growth
- Community
- Finding Meaning

My Faith:

Use this section for a card reading, bible verse or quote that speaks to you.

My Journaling

Wednesday 12 May to Wednesday 19 May 2021 - Southern
Tuesday 11 May to Wednesday 19 May 2021 - Northern

Mercury in Retrograde: Pre: 14 to 30 May in Gemini

New Moon
Wed 12 May
Tues 11 May

Journaling prompt: Write a letter to someone who believed in you even when you didn't believe in yourself.

First Quarter Moon Power Up

Moving Forward

Thursday 20 May 2021 – Southern
Wednesday 19 May 2021 – Northern

What actions will you take now to move your intentions forward?

- Physical Health
- Mental and Cognitive Health
- Abundance and Lifestyle
- Safety and Security
- Environment
- Play
- Authenticity
- Communication
- Relationships
- Self-Responsibility and Growth
- Community
- Finding Meaning

My Journaling

Thursday 20 May to Tuesday 25 May 2021 - Southern
Wednesday 19 May to Tuesday 25 May 2021 – Northern

Mercury in Retrograde: Pre: 14 to 30 May in Gemini

First Quarter Moon
Thurs 20 May
Wed 19 May

Journaling prompt: What would you do if you knew you could not fail?

Full Moon Celebration

The Harvest
Wednesday 26 May 2021 **Super Moon** – Southern
Wednesday 26 May 2021 **Super Moon** – Northern

Total Lunar Eclipse (Blood Moon) in Sagittarius
A need for more freedom, adventure, travel, and change.
Can be seen from Australia, parts of west US, west South America, or South-East Asia

What am I celebrating and reaping the harvest of this Full Moon?

- ☯ Physical Health
- ☯ Mental and cognitive Health
- ☯ Abundance and lifestyle
- ☯ Safety and Security
- ☯ Environment
- ☯ Play
- ☯ Authenticity
- ☯ Communication
- ☯ Relationships
- ☯ Self-Responsibility and Growth
- ☯ Community
- ☯ Finding Meaning

The full moon in May

The Frost Moon in the **Southern Hemisphere;** by this time of the year it begins to turn to winter. Autumn has arrived and the air is chilled during the day and cold during the night.

The Flower Moon in the **Northern Hemisphere;** is the time of flowers bloom after the April rains.

My Journaling

Wednesday 26 May to Tuesday 1 June 2021 - Southern
Wednesday 26 May to Tuesday 1 June 2021 - Northern

Mercury in Retrograde: Pre: 14 to 30 May in Gemini,
Full: 31 May to 23 June in Gemini

Full Moon
Wed 26 May

Journaling prompt: What qualities do you want in a romantic partner?

Third Quarter Moon Releasing

Letting It Go
Wednesday 2 June 2021 – Southern
Wednesday 2 June 2021 – Northern

At this time of the Third Quarter Moon I see, acknowledge and release...

- Physical Health
- Mental and Cognitive Health
- Abundance and Lifestyle
- Safety and Security
- Environment
- Play
- Authenticity
- Communication
- Relationships
- Self-Responsibility and Growth
- Community
- Finding Meaning

My Journaling

Wednesday 2 June to Friday 9 June 2021 - Southern
Wednesday 2 June to Friday 9 June 2021 - Northern

Mercury in Retrograde: Full: 31 Mat to 23 June in Gemini

Third Quarter
Moon
Wed 2 June

Journaling prompt: What are you best at, and what do you love doing most, and how could you

spend more time doing both?

Lunar Cycle 5

Thursday 10 June Friday 9 July 2021

New Moon Manifesting

New Beginnings
Saturday 10 June 2021 – Southern
Saturday 10 June 2021 – Northern

What are your intentions for the coming lunar cycle?

- Physical Health
- Mental and Cognitive Health
- Abundance and Lifestyle
- Safety and Security
- Environment
- Play
- Authenticity
- Communication
- Relationships
- Self-Responsibility and Growth
- Community
- Finding Meaning

My Faith:
Use this section for a card reading, bible verse or quote that speaks to you.

My Journaling

Saturday 10 June to Thursday 17 June 2021 - Southern
Saturday 10 June to Thursday 17 June 2021 - Northern

Mercury in Retrograde: Full: 31 Mat to 23 June in Gemini

New Moon
Sat 10 June

Journaling prompt: If you had a magic wand, and could wave away your problems, what would

your life look like? What's stopping you from being the wand?

First Quarter Moon Power Up

Moving Forward
Friday 18 June 2021 – Southern
Friday 18 June 2021 – Northern

What actions will you take now to move your intentions forward?

- Physical Health
- Mental and Cognitive Health
- Abundance and Lifestyle
- Safety and Security
- Environment
- Play
- Authenticity
- Communication
- Relationships
- Self-Responsibility and Growth
- Community
- Finding Meaning

My Journaling

Friday 18 June to Thursday 24 June 2021 - Southern
Friday 18 June to Thursday 24 June 2021 – Northern

Mercury in Retrograde: Full: 31 May to 23 June in Gemini
Post: 24 June to 12 July in Gemini

First Quarter Moon
Fri 18 June

Journaling prompt: Where do you see yourself in 3 months, 6 months, and 12 months? Be specific

Full Moon Celebration

The Harvest
Friday 25 June 2021 – Southern
Thursday 24 June 2021 – Northern

What am I celebrating and reaping the harvest of this Full Moon?

- Physical Health
- Mental and Cognitive Health
- Abundance and Lifestyle
- Safety and Security
- Environment
- Pl...
- Authenticity
- Communication
- Relationships
- Self-Responsibility and Growth
- Community
- Finding Meaning

The full moon in June

The Long Night or Dingo Moon in the **Southern Hemisphere;** the midwinter moon rises high across the sky and is opposite a low Sun, bringing about the longest nights of the year. In Australia this month also marks the end of the Dingo breeding cycle and the first litters are appearing.

The Rose or Strawberry Moon in the **Northern Hemisphere;** is when strawberries are blooming, the French call this moon la lune rose, which translates into English as 'the rose moon'

My Journaling

Friday 25 June to Thursday 1 July 2021 - Southern
Thursday 24 June to Thursday 1 July 2021 - Northern

Mercury in Retrograde: Post: 24 June to 12 July in Gemini

20 to 23 June
Winter Solstice - Alban Arthan, - Southern,
Summer Solstice - Alban Hefin, - Northern

Full Moon
Fri 25 June
Thurs 24 June

Journaling prompt: What would you tell your five-year-old self?

Third Quarter Moon Releasing

Letting It Go
Friday 2 July 2021 – Southern
Thursday 1 July 2021 – Northern

At this time of the Third Quarter Moon I see, acknowledge and release...

- Physical Health
- Mental and Cognitive Health
- Abundance and Lifestyle
- Safety and Security
- Environment
- Play
- Authenticity
- Communication
- Relationships
- Self-Responsibility and Growth
- Community
- Finding Meaning

My Journaling

Friday 2 July to Friday 9 July 2021 - Southern
Thursday 1 July to Friday 9 July 2021 - Northern

Mercury in Retrograde: Post: 24 June to 12 July in Gemini

Third Quarter
Moon
Fri 2 July
Thurs 1 July

Journaling prompt: Nobody knows that 1 . . .

Lunar Cycle 6

Saturday 10 July to Saturday 7 August 2021

New Moon Manifesting

New Beginnings
Saturday 10 July 2021 – Southern
Saturday 10 July 2021 – Northern

What are your intentions for the coming lunar cycle?

- Physical Health
- Mental and Cognitive Health
- Abundance and Lifestyle
- Safety and Security
- Environment
- Play
- Authenticity
- Communication
- Relationships
- Self-Responsibility and Growth
- Community
- Finding Meaning

My Faith:

Use this section for a card reading, bible verse or quote that speaks to you.

My Journaling

Saturday 10 July to Friday 16 July January 2021 - Southern
Saturday 10 July to Friday 16 July 2021 - Northern

Mercury in Retrograde: Post: 24 June to 12 July in Gemini

New Moon
Sat 10 July

Journaling prompt: Who do you need to forgive, and why, and what's stopping you from doing it today?

First Quarter Moon Power Up

Moving Forward
Saturday 17 July 2021 – Southern
Saturday 17 July 2021 – Northern

What actions will you take now to move your intentions forward?

- Physical Health
- Mental and Cognitive Health
- Abundance and Lifestyle
- Safety and Security
- Environment
- Play
- Authenticity
- Communication
- Relationships
- Self-Responsibility and Growth
- Community
- Finding Meaning

My Journaling

Saturday 17 July to Friday 23 July 2021 - Southern
Saturday 17 July to Friday 23 July 2021 – Northern

First Quarter Moon
Sat 17 July

Journaling prompt: What are you the most scared of losing, and what would you truly lose if you lost it?

Full Moon Celebration

The Harvest
Saturday 24 July 2021 – Southern
Saturday 24 July 2021 – Northern

What am I celebrating and reaping the harvest of this Full Moon?

- Physical Health
- Mental and Cognitive Health
- Abundance and Lifestyle
- Safety and Security
- Environment
- Play
- Authenticity
- Communication
- Relationships
- Self-Responsibility and Growth
- Community
- Finding Meaning

The full moon in July

The Winter Moon in the **Southern Hemisphere** is the time when the build up to winter has passed and cold has settled in.

The Buck Moon in the **Northern Hemisphere;** the moose and the dear are growing and the bucks grow their first antlers during this month.

My Journaling

Saturday 24 July to Friday 30 July 2021 - Southern
Saturday 24 July to Friday 30 July 2021 - Northern

Full Moon
Sat 24 July

Journaling prompt: What do you love most about yourself?

Third Quarter Moon Releasing

Letting It Go

Saturday 31 July 2021 – Southern
Saturday 31 July 2021 – Northern

At this time of the Third Quarter Moon I see, acknowledge and release...

- Physical Health
- Mental and Cognitive Health
- Abundance and Lifestyle
- Safety and Security
- Environment
- Play
- Authenticity
- Communication
- Relationships
- Self-Responsibility and Growth
- Community
- Finding Meaning

My Journaling

Saturday 31 July to Saturday 7 August 2021 - Southern
Saturday 31 July to Saturday 7 August 2021 - Northern

Third Quarter
Moon
Sat 31 July

Journaling prompt: What about your life makes you the most proud?

Lunar Cycle 7

Sunday 8 August to Monday 6 September 2021

New Moon Manifesting

New Beginnings
Sunday 8 August 2021 – Southern
Sunday 8 August 2021 – Northern

What are your intentions for the coming lunar cycle?

- Physical Health
- Mental and Cognitive Health
- Abundance and Lifestyle
- Safety and Security
- Environment
- Play
- Authenticity
- Communication
- Relationships
- Self-Responsibility and Growth
- Community
- Finding Meaning

My Faith:

Use this section for a card reading, bible verse or quote that speaks to you.

My Journaling

Sunday 8 August to Sunday 15 August 2021 - Southern
Sunday 8 August to Sunday 15 August 2021 - Northern

New Moon
Sun 8 Aug

Journaling prompt: What does heroic mean to you, and who are your biggest heroes?

First Quarter Moon Power Up

Moving Forward

Monday 16 August 2021 – Southern
Monday 16 August 2021 – Northern

What actions will you take now to move your intentions forward?

- Physical Health
- Mental and Cognitive Health
- Abundance and Lifestyle
- Safety and Security
- Environment
- Play
- Authenticity
- Communication
- Relationships
- Self-Responsibility and Growth
- Community
- Finding Meaning

My Journaling

Monday 16 August to Saturday 21 August 2021 - Southern
Monday 16 August to Saturday 21 August 2021 – Northern

First Quarter Moon
Mon 16 Aug

Journaling prompt: What do you love most about your life?

Full Moon Celebration

The Harvest
Sunday 22 August 2021 – Southern
Sunday 22 August 2021 – Northern

What am I celebrating and reaping the harvest of this Full Moon?

- Physical Health
- Mental and Cognitive Health
- Abundance and Lifestyle
- Safety and Security
- Environment
- Authenticity
- Communication
- Relationships
- Self-Responsibility and Growth
- Community
- Finding Meaning

The full moon in August

The Kangaroo Moon in the **Southern Hemisphere**; kangaroo and wallaby joeys emerge from their safe and warm pouches as they start exploring their environment.

The Green Corn Moon in the **Northern Hemisphere**; the time when the crops start to ripen ready for harvest

My Journaling

Sunday 22 August to Sunday 29 August 2021 - Southern
Sunday 22 August to Sunday 29 August 2021 - Northern

Full Moon
Sun 22 Aug

Journaling prompt: If you found out that you were going to die tomorrow,

what would be your three biggest regrets?

Third Quarter Moon Releasing

Letting It Go

Monday 30 August 2021 – Southern
Monday 30 August 2021 – Northern

At this time of the Third Quarter Moon I see, acknowledge and release...

- Physical Health
- Mental and Cognitive Health
- Abundance and Lifestyle
- Safety and Security
- Environment
- Play
- Authenticity
- Communication
- Relationships
- Self-Responsibility and Growth
- Community
- Finding Meaning

My Journaling

Monday 30 August to Monday 6 September 2021 - Southern
Monday 30 August to Monday 6 September 2021 - Northern

Mercury in Retrograde: Pre: 6 to 27 September in Libra

Third Quarter
Moon
Mon 30 Aug

Journaling prompt: What makes you feel happy to be alive, and how can you make more of that every day?

Lunar Cycle 8

Tuesday 7 September to Tuesday 5 October 2021

New Moon Manifesting

New Beginnings
Tuesday 7 September 2021 – Southern
Tuesday 7 September 2021 – Northern

What are your intentions for the coming lunar cycle?

- Physical Health
- Mental and Cognitive Health
- Abundance and Lifestyle
- Safety and Security
- Environment
- Play
- Authenticity
- Communication
- Relationships
- Self-Responsibility and Growth
- Community
- Finding Meaning

My Faith:

Use this section for a card reading, bible verse or quote that speaks to you.

My Journaling

Tuesday 7 September to Monday 13 September 2021 - Southern
Tuesday 7 September to Monday 13 September 2021 - Northern

Mercury in Retrograde: Pre: 6 to 27 September in Libra

New Moon
Tues 7 Sept

Journaling prompt: What did you really love doing as a kid but don't really do anymore? What is

stopping you from doing it now, and what would happen if you did?

First Quarter Moon Power Up

Moving Forward

Tuesday 14 September 2021 – Southern
Tuesday 14 September 2021 – Northern

What actions will you take now to move your intentions forward?

- Physical Health
- Mental and Cognitive Health
- Abundance and Lifestyle
- Safety and Security
- Environment
- Play
- Authenticity
- Communication
- Relationships
- Self-Responsibility and Growth
- Community
- Finding Meaning

My Journaling

Tuesday 14 September to Monday 20 September 2021 - Southern
Tuesday 14 September to Monday 20 September 2021 – Northern

Mercury in Retrograde: Pre: 6 to 27 September in Libra

First Quarter Moon
Tues 14 Sept

Journaling prompt: What are the five most important things in your life right now and how are you prioritizing them (or not)?

Full Moon Celebration

The Harvest

Tuesday 21 September 2021 – Southern
Tuesday 21 September 2021 – Northern

What am I celebrating and reaping the harvest of this Full Moon?

- Physical Health
- Mental and Cognitive Health
- Abundance and Lifestyle
- Safety and Security
- Environment
- Play
- Authenticity
- Communication
- Relationships
- Self-Responsibility and Growth
- Community
- Finding Meaning

The full moon in September

The Fish Moon in the **Southern Hemisphere;** is the pre-monsoon season and the humidity is on the rise. That makes for good fishing weather and is also the pre-breeding season for fish with many on the run to their ancestral breeding grounds.

The Harvest Moon in the **Northern Hemisphere;** provides extra light for the long days of harvesting

My Journaling

Tuesday 21 September to Tuesday 28 September 2021 - Southern
Tuesday 21 September to Tuesday 28 September 2021 - Northern

Mercury in Retrograde: Pre: 6 to 27 September in Libra

20 to 23 September
Spring Equinox - Alban Eilir - Southern
Autumn Equinox - Alban Elfed,- Northern

Full Moon
Tues 21 Sept

Journaling prompt: When was the last time you cried, and what did it teach you?

Third Quarter Moon Releasing

Letting It Go
Wednesday 29 September 2021 – Southern
Wednesday 29 September 2021 – Northern

At this time of the Third Quarter Moon I see, acknowledge and release...

- Physical Health
- Mental and Cognitive Health
- Abundance and Lifestyle
- Safety and Security
- Environment
- Play
- Authenticity
- Communication
- Relationships
- Self-Responsibility and Growth
- Community
- Finding Meaning

My Journaling

Wednesday 29 September to Tuesday 5 October 2021 - Southern
Wednesday 29 September to Tuesday 5 October 2021 - Northern

Mercury in Retrograde: Full: 28 September to 19 October in Libra

Third Quarter
Moon
Wed 29 Sept

Journaling prompt: What does your ideal day look like? Be specific.

Lunar Cycle 9

Wednesday 6 October to Thursday 4 November 2021

New Moon Manifesting

New Beginnings
Wednesday 6 October 2021 – Southern
Wednesday 6 October 2021 – Northern

What are your intentions for the coming lunar cycle?

- Physical Health
- Mental and Cognitive Health
- Abundance and Lifestyle
- Safety and Security
- Environment
- Play
- Authenticity
- Communication
- Relationships
- Self-Responsibility and Growth
- Community
- Finding Meaning

My Faith:
Use this section for a card reading, bible verse or quote that speaks to you.

My Journaling

Wednesday 6 October to Tuesday 12 October 2021 - Southern
Wednesday 6 October to Tuesday 12 October 2021 - Northern

Mercury in Retrograde: Full: 28 September to 19 October in Libra

New Moon
Wed 6 Oct

Journaling prompt: What is something you have never done, but always wanted to do, and what is

so important about this for you?

First Quarter Moon Power Up

Moving Forward
Wednesday 13 October 2021 – Southern
Wednesday 13 October 2021 – Northern

What actions will you take now to move your intentions forward?

- Physical Health
- Mental and Cognitive Health
- Abundance and Lifestyle
- Safety and Security
- Environment
- Play
- Authenticity
- Communication
- Relationships
- Self-Responsibility and Growth
- Community
- Finding Meaning

My Journaling

Wednesday 13 October to Wednesday 20 October 2021 - Southern
Wednesday 13 October to Wednesday 20 October 2021 – Northern

Mercury n Retrograde: Full: 28 September to 19 October in Libra,
Post: 20 October to 2 November in Libra

First Quarter Moon
Wed 13 Oct

Journaling prompt: What does it mean to be good enough, and how do you know that you are?

Full Moon Celebration

The Harvest
Thursday 21 October 2021 – Southern
Wednesday 20 October 2021 – Northern

What am I celebrating and reaping the harvest of this Full Moon?

- Physical Health
- Mental and Cognitive Health
- Abundance and Lifestyle
- Safety and Security
- Environment
- Pl...
- Authenticity
- Communication
- Relationships
- Self-Responsibility and Growth
- Community
- Finding Meaning

The full moon in October

The Pink Moon in the **Southern Hemisphere;** carries this name from the herb moss pink, or wild ground phlox, which is one of the earliest widespread flowers of the spring.

The Hunters Moon in the **Northern Hemisphere;** is the prime time to hunt post-harvest and pre-winter when conditions were optimal for spotting prey.

My Journaling

Thursday 21 October to Thursday 28 October 2021 - Southern
Wednesday 20 October to Thursday 28 October 2021 - Northern

Mercury in Retrograde: Post: 20 October to 2 November in Libra

Full Moon
Thurs 21 Oct
Wed 20 Oct

Journaling prompt: What makes you the most angry, the most frustrated,

the most annoyed, and why?

Third Quarter Moon Releasing

Letting It Go

Friday 29 October 2021 – Southern
Thursday 28 October 2021 – Northern

At this time of the Third Quarter Moon I see, acknowledge and release...

- Physical Health
- Mental and Cognitive Health
- Abundance and Lifestyle
- Safety and Security
- Environment
- Play
- Authenticity
- Communication
- Relationships
- Self-Responsibility and Growth
- Community
- Finding Meaning

My Journaling

Friday 29 October to Thursday 4 November 2021 - Southern
Thursday 28 October to Thursday 4 November 2021 - Northern

Mercury in Retrograde: Post: 20 October to 2 November in Libra

31 October
Beltane, the beginning of Summer - Southern
Samhain (Halloween), the beginning of Winter - Northern

Third Quarter Moon
Fri 29 Oct
Thurs 28 Oct

Journaling prompt: How can you improve the way you treat yourself and talk to yourself?

Lunar Cycle 10

Friday 5 November to Friday 3 December 2021

New Moon Manifesting

New Beginnings
Friday 5 November 2021 – Southern
Friday 5 November 2021 – Northern

What are your intentions for the coming lunar cycle?

- ☯ Physical Health
- ☯ Mental and Cognitive Health
- ☯ Abundance and Lifestyle
- ☯ Safety and Security
- ☯ Environment
- ☯ Play
- ☯ Authenticity
- ☯ Communication
- ☯ Relationships
- ☯ Self-Responsibility and Growth
- ☯ Community
- ☯ Finding Meaning

My Faith:

Use this section for a card reading, bible verse or quote that speaks to you.

My Journaling

Friday 5 November to Wednesday 10 November 2021 - Southern
Friday 5 November to Wednesday 10 November 2021 - Northern

New Moon
Fri 5 Nov

Journaling prompt: Write whatever is in your head, it could be a menu, a to do list or a journal

entry, a story, a poem or just a dumping of thoughts.
(This exercise is known as "Morning Pages" from Julia Cameron's The Artists Way)

First Quarter Moon Power Up

Moving Forward
Thursday 11 November 2021 – Southern
Thursday 11 November 2021 – Northern

What actions will you take now to move your intentions forward?

- Physical Health
- Mental and Cognitive Health
- Abundance and Lifestyle
- Safety and Security
- Environment
- Play
- Authenticity
- Communication
- Relationships
- Self-Responsibility and Growth
- Community
- Finding Meaning

My Journaling

Thursday 11 November to Thursday 18 November 2021 - Southern
Thursday 11 November to Thursday 18 November 2021 – Northern

First Quarter Moon
Thurs 11 Nov

Journaling prompt: Make a list of 30 things that make you smile.

Full Moon Celebration

The Harvest
Friday 19 November 2021 – Southern
Friday 19 November 2021 – Northern

Partial Lunar Eclipse in Taurus
Can be seen North and South America, Australia, and parts of Europe and Asia

What am I celebrating and reaping the harvest of this Full Moon?

- Physical Health
- Mental and Cognitive Health
- Abundance and Lifestyle
- Safety and Security
- Environment
- Play
- Authenticity
- Communication
- Relationships
- Self-Responsibility and Growth
- Community
- Finding Meaning

The full moon in November

The Wild Flower Moon in the **Southern Hemisphere;** is Spring time as Mother Nature begins to wake from her cold sleep. With plants in general in full bloom by November.

The Beaver Moon in the **Northern Hemisphere;** traps were once set in this month to catch enough beaver to make warm clothing for the upcoming winter.

My Journaling

Friday 19 November to Friday 26 November 2021 - Southern
Friday 19 November to Friday 26 November 2021 - Northern

Full Moon
Fri 19 Nov

Journaling prompt: I really wish others knew this about me...

Third Quarter Moon Releasing

Letting It Go

Saturday 27 November 2021 – Southern
Saturday 27 November 2021 – Northern

At this time of the Third Quarter Moon I see, acknowledge and release...

- Physical Health
- Mental and Cognitive Health
- Abundance and Lifestyle
- Safety and Security
- Environment
- Play
- Authenticity
- Communication
- Relationships
- Self-Responsibility and Growth
- Community
- Finding Meaning

My Journaling

Saturday 27 November to Friday 3 December 2021 - Southern
Saturday 27 November to Friday 3 December 2021 - Northern

Third Quarter
Moon
Sat 27 Nov

Journaling prompt: Name what is enough for you.

Lunar Cycle 11

Saturday 4 December to Saturday 2 January 2022

New Moon Manifesting

New Beginnings
Saturday 4 December 2021 – Southern
Saturday 4 December 2021 – Northern

What are your intentions for the coming lunar cycle?

- Physical Health
- Mental and Cognitive Health
- Abundance and Lifestyle
- Safety and Security
- Environment
- Play
- Authenticity
- Communication
- Relationships
- Self-Responsibility and Growth
- Community
- Finding Meaning

My Faith:

Use this section for a card reading, bible verse or quote that speaks to you.

My Journaling

Saturday 4 December to Friday 10 December 2021 - Southern
Saturday 4 December to Friday 10 December 2021 – Northern

First Quarter Moon
Sat 4 Dec

Journaling prompt: What always brings tears to your eyes?

(As Paulo Coelho has said, "Tears are words that need to be written.")

First Quarter Moon Power Up

Moving Forward
Saturday 11 December 2021 – Southern
Saturday 11 December 2021 – Northern

What actions will you take now to move your intentions forward?

- Physical Health
- Mental and Cognitive Health
- Abundance and Lifestyle
- Safety and Security
- Environment
- Play
- Authenticity
- Communication
- Relationships
- Self-Responsibility and Growth
- Community
- Finding Meaning

My Journaling

Saturday 11 December to Saturday 18 December 2021 - Southern
Saturday 11 December to Saturday 18 December 2021 – Northern

First Quarter Moon
Sat 11 Dec

Journaling prompt: Name a compassionate way you've supported a friend recently. Then write

down how you can do the same for yourself.

Full Moon Celebration

The Harvest
Sunday 19 December 2021 – Southern
Sunday 19 December 2021 – Northern

What am I celebrating and reaping the harvest of this Full Moon?

- Physical Health
- Mental and Cognitive Health
- Abundance and Lifestyle
- Safety and Security
- Environment
- Pl
- Authenticity
- Communication
- Relationships
- Self-Responsibility and Growth
- Community
- Finding Meaning

The full moon in December

The Swan Moon in the **Southern Hemisphere;** is the time black swans move in large numbers to the sheltered waters as the freshwater wetlands dry up.

The Cold Moon in the **Northern Hemisphere;** is the month when winter truly begins, also called the Moon Before Yule, which is the ancient celebration around the winter solstice

My Journaling

Sunday 19 December to Sunday 26 December 2021 - Southern
Sunday 19 December to Sunday 26 December 2021 - Northern

20 to 23 December
Summer Solstice - Alban Hefin, - Southern
Winter Solstice - Alban Arthan - Northern

Full Moon
Sun 19 Dec

Journaling prompt: Make a list of everything that inspires you — from books to websites to

quotes to people to paintings to stores to the stars.

Third Quarter Moon Releasing

Letting It Go

Monday 27 December 2021 – Southern
Monday 27 December 2021 – Northern

At this time of the Third Quarter Moon I see, acknowledge and release...

- Physical Health
- Mental and Cognitive Health
- Abundance and Lifestyle
- Safety and Security
- Environment
- Play
- Authenticity
- Communication
- Relationships
- Self-Responsibility and Growth
- Community
- Finding Meaning

My Journaling

Monday 27 December to Friday 2 January 2022 - Southern
Monday 27 December to Friday 2 January 2022 - Northern

Mercury in Retrograde: Pre: 28 December to 14 January in Aquarius

Third Quarter
Moon
Mon 27 Dec

Journaling prompt: Dear __, it weighs on me that I never told you . . .

Lunar Cycle 12

Sunday 3 January to Sunday 31 January 2022

New Moon Manifesting

New Beginnings
Sunday 3 January 2022 – Southern
Sunday 3 January 2022 – Northern

What are your intentions for the coming lunar cycle?

- Physical Health
- Mental and Cognitive Health
- Abundance and Lifestyle
- Safety and Security
- Environment
- Play
- Authenticity
- Communication
- Relationships
- Self-Responsibility and Growth
- Community
- Finding Meaning

My Faith:
Use this section for a card reading, bible verse or quote that speaks to you.

My Journaling

Sunday 3 January to Saturday 9 January 2022 - Southern
Sunday 3 January to Saturday 9 January 2022 - Northern

Mercury in Retrograde: Pre: 28 December to 14 January in Aquarius

New Moon
Sun 3 Jan

Journaling prompt: If you could become an expert in any subject or activity, what would it be?

First Quarter Moon Power Up

Moving Forward
Sunday 10 January 2022 – Southern
Sunday 10 January 2022 – Northern

What actions will you take now to move your intentions forward?

- Physical Health
- Mental and Cognitive Health
- Abundance and Lifestyle
- Safety and Security
- Environment
- Play
- Authenticity
- Communication
- Relationships
- Self-Responsibility and Growth
- Community
- Finding Meaning

My Journaling

Sunday 10 January to Sunday 17 January 2022 - Southern
Sunday 10 January to Sunday 17 January 2022 – Northern

Mercury in Retrograde: Pre: 28 December to 14 January in Aquarius,
Full: 15 January to 5 February in Aquarius

First Quarter Moon
Sun 10 Jan

Journaling prompt: What makes your heart sing loudest? What makes your heart beat strongest?

Full Moon Celebration

The Harvest

Monday 18 January 2022 – Southern
Sunday 17 January 2022 – Northern

What am I celebrating and reaping the harvest of this Full Moon?

- Physical Health
- Mental and Cognitive Health
- Abundance and Lifestyle
- Safety and Security
- Environment
- Play
- Authenticity
- Communication
- Relationships
- Self-Responsibility and Growth
- Community
- Finding Meaning

The full moon in January

The Thunder Moon in the **Southern Hemisphere;** is the time thunderstorms are most frequent. This first full moon in the calendar year could also be called the Rumble Moon or the Lightning Moon.

The Hunger Moon in the **Northern Hemisphere;** in cold and temperate climates, it was difficult to find food during January, thus the name hunger moon.

My Journaling

Monday 18 January to Monday 25 January 2022 - Southern
Sunday 17 January to Monday 25 January 2022 - Northern

Mercury in Retrograde: Full: 15 January to 5 February in Aquarius

Full Moon
Mon 18 Jan
Sun 17 Jan

Journaling prompt: If you were unapologetically and truly yourself, day in and day out, and if you

fully accepted and loved yourself, what would change for you moving forward?

Third Quarter Moon Releasing

Letting It Go
Tuesday 26 January 2022 – Southern
Monday 25 January 2022 – Northern

At this time of the Third Quarter Moon I see, acknowledge and release...

- Physical Health
- Mental and Cognitive Health
- Abundance and Lifestyle
- Safety and Security
- Environment
- Play
- Authenticity
- Communication
- Relationships
- Self-Responsibility and Growth
- Community
- Finding Meaning

My Journaling

Tuesday 26 January to Sunday 31 January 2022 - Southern
Monday 25 January to Sunday 31 January 2022 - Northern

Mercury in Retrograde: Full: 15 January to 5 February in Aquarius

Third Quarter Moon
Tues 26 Jan
Mon 25 Jan

Journaling prompt: What scares you the most, and why?

How can you use that fear to improve or learn or grow?

Lunar Cycle 13

Monday 1 February to Tuesday 1 March 2022

New Moon Manifesting

New Beginnings
Monday 1 February 2022 – Southern
Monday 1 February 2022 – Northern

What are your intentions for the coming lunar cycle?

- ☯ Physical Health
- ☯ Mental and Cognitive Health
- ☯ Abundance and Lifestyle
- ☯ Safety and Security
- ☯ Environment
- ☯ Play
- ☯ Authenticity
- ☯ Communication
- ☯ Relationships
- ☯ Self-Responsibility and Growth
- ☯ Community
- ☯ Finding Meaning

My Faith:
Use this section for a card reading, bible verse or quote that speaks to you.

My Journaling

Monday 1 February to Monday 8 February 2022 - Southern
Monday 1 February to Monday 8 February 2022 - Northern

Mercury in Retrograde: Full: 15 January to 5 February in Aquarius

New Moon
Mon 1 Feb

Journaling prompt: What are three things that you are really looking forward to the most?

First Quarter Moon Power Up

Moving Forward
Tuesday 9 February 2022 – Southern
Monday 8 February 2022 – Northern

What actions will you take now to move your intentions forward?

- Physical Health
- Mental and Cognitive Health
- Abundance and Lifestyle
- Safety and Security
- Environment
- Play
- Authenticity
- Communication
- Relationships
- Self-Responsibility and Growth
- Community
- Finding Meaning

My Journaling

Tuesday 9 February to Tuesday 16 February 2022 - Southern
Monday 8 February to Tuesday 16 February 2022 – Northern

Mercury in Retrograde: Post: 6 to 27 February in Aquarius

First Quarter Moon
Tues 9 Feb
Mon 8 Feb

Journaling prompt: How do you deal with helplessness, with letting go, with release and surrender

of expectations?

Full Moon Celebration

The Harvest
Wednesday 17 February 2022 – Southern
Tuesday 16 February 2022 – Northern

What am I celebrating and reaping the harvest of this Full Moon?

- Physical Health
- Mental and Cognitive Health
- Abundance and Lifestyle
- Safety and Security
- Environment
- Play
- Authenticity
- Communication
- Relationships
- Self-Responsibility and Growth
- Community
- Finding Meaning

The full moon in February

The Red Moon in the **Southern Hemisphere;** rises in February, often appearing reddish through a scorching haze of summer heat.

The Snow Moon in the **Northern Hemisphere;** appears when the snow is deepest, thus this is a time for home, hearth and family.

My Journaling

Wednesday 17 February to Tuesday 23 February 2022 - Southern
Tuesday 16 February to Tuesday 23 February 2022 - Northern

Mercury in Retrograde: Post: 6 to 27 February in Aquarius

Full Moon
Wed 17 Feb
Tues 16 Feb

Journaling prompt: When did you hurt most, and how has it helped you or taught you or

improved you?

Third Quarter Moon Releasing

Letting It Go

Wednesday 24 February 2022 – Southern
Tuesday 23 February 2022 – Northern

At this time of the Third Quarter Moon I see, acknowledge and release...

- Physical Health
- Mental and Cognitive Health
- Abundance and Lifestyle
- Safety and Security
- Environment
- Play
- Authenticity
- Communication
- Relationships
- Self-Responsibility and Growth
- Community
- Finding Meaning

My Journaling

Wednesday 24 February to Tuesday 1 March 2022 - Southern
Tuesday 23 February to Tuesday 1 March 2022 - Northern

Mercury in Retrograde: Post: 6 to 27 February in Aquarius

Third Quarter Moon
Wed 24 Feb
Tues 23 Feb

Journaling prompt: What are five things that you love most in the world?

CPSIA information can be obtained
at www.ICGtesting.com
Printed in the USA
BVHW060802021120
592323BV00014B/283